**SpeakEasy Communications, Inc.**
The Nation's Leader in Survival Spanish
Changing Attitudes & Abilities Since 1997™

D1616577

# SpeakEasy's

# Survival Spanish
# for
# All Americans

Myelita Melton, MA

HILLSBORO PUBLIC LIBRARIES
WITHDRAWN
Member of Washington County
COOPERATIVE LIBRARY SERVICES

Survival Spanish for All Americans

Author: Myelita A. Melton
Cover illustration: Ellen Wass Beckerman
Published by SpeakEasy Communications, Inc.
116 Sea Trail Drive
Mooresville, NC 28117-8493
USA

ISBN    0-9712593-9-9 38516810    9/08

©2006 SpeakEasy Communications, Incorporated. All rights reserved.
No part of this guide may be duplicated or reproduced, stored in a retrieval system, or transmitted, in any form or by any means, electronic, mechanical, recording, or otherwise, without the express written consent of the author.

Survival Spanish for All Americans, SpeakEasy Spanish, and SpeakEasySpanish.com are either trademarks or registered trademarks of SpeakEasy Communications, Inc. in the United States and/or other countries.

The content of this book is furnished for informational use only, is subject to change without notice, and should not be construed as a commitment by SpeakEasy Communications, Incorporated. SpeakEasy Communications, Incorporated assumes no responsibility or liability for any errors, omissions, or inaccuracies that may appear in the informational content contained in this guide.

# Foreword

I started learning Spanish at seventeen, and I think it's one of the best decisions I've ever made. It happened by accident, but I don't think it was a coincidence. In my senior year of high school I just decided to take Spanish instead of Physics; the sciences were never my thing. On the first day of class I was hooked. The sound of Spanish spoke to my soul, and I knew I had made the right decision. For the next year, I begged my parents to let me take my savings and go to Mexico to study. They thought it was a crazy phase I was going through and it would pass eventually. It didn't. Three days after high school graduation I flew to Mexico for the first time. ¡Muchas gracias, Mom and Dad! Since high school, Spanish has always been a part of my life and it always will be. I'm glad that you are making Spanish a part of your life, too.

Spanish hasn't always come easy to me. There have been plenty of times when I couldn't remember the right word- or any word for that matter. I've also made my share of mistakes, and I'm sure I always will. No matter what, I can say that knowing Spanish has rewarded me richly. It's brought me great friends I would never have had, and it's taken me places I would have never been brave enough to go. But best of all, it's given me a greater understanding of Latinos, the most fascinating people on our planet! So, this book is dedicated to you, one of the millions of Americans who want to reach out and make connections with neighbors, friends, colleagues, and customers who speak Spanish. I've loaded it with what I consider to be the essential things that all Americans should know about one of the most beautiful and expressive languages in the world. ¡Buena suerte, amigos!

# Table of Contents
Survival Spanish for All Americans

# Using This Material

Welcome to *SpeakEasy's Survival Spanish* ™. This material is for adults with no previous experience in the Spanish language. Through research and interviews with professionals in your field, we have developed this material to be a practical guide to using Spanish on the job. Wherever possible, we have chosen to use the similarities between English and Spanish to facilitate your success.

Throughout the manual you will find study tips and pronunciation guides that will help you to say the words correctly. In the guides, we have broken down the Spanish words for you by syllables, choosing English words that closely approximate the Spanish sound needed. This makes learning Spanish more accessible because it doesn't seem so foreign. When you see letters that are **BOLD** in the guide, say that part of the word the loudest. The bold capital letters are there to show you where the emphasis falls in that particular word.

At SpeakEasy Communications, we believe that *communication* is more important than *conjugation*, and we urge you to set realistic, practical goals for learning. Make practice a regular part of your day and you will be surprised at the progress you make!

# LATIN AMERICA

## What's The Proper Term?
## Both!

**Latino/Latina**: Anyone from Latin America who speaks Spanish as his or her native language. (Preferred)

**Hispanic**: Anyone who speaks Spanish as his or her native language and traces family origin to Spain.

**Note**: Don't assume that because a person speaks Spanish that they are Mexican. They could be from anywhere in Latin America

---

**Hispanics in America come mainly from the following three countries:**

1. **Mexico**
2. **Cuba**
3. **Puerto Rico**

*Central America*

**Many Latinos from El Salvador, Honduras and Guatemala are coming to America because of Hurricane Mitch in 1998.**

**According to US Census:**

1. There are over 43 million in the US, who speak Spanish.
2. Hispanics are now the majority minority in America (12.7%).
3. By 2050 Hispanics will make up 25% of the US population.
4. Georgia & NC have the fastest growing Hispanic populations.
5. Over 17% of the nation's school-aged children are Latino.
6. Latino buying power surged this year to over 700 billion dollars.
7. 47% are limited in English proficiency.
8. 27% of Latinos over the age of 25 complete the 9th grade.

# SpeakEasy's Secrets to Learning Spanish

***Congratulations on your decision to learn to speak Spanish!*** This is one of the smartest choices you will ever make considering the increasing diversity in our country. It's definitely a decision you will never regret. You are now among a growing number of America's visionary leaders, who want to build better, stronger relationships with Latin Americans, the fastest growing segment of the American workforce.

Learning Spanish is going to open many doors for you, and it will affect you in ways that you can't even imagine. By learning Spanish, you will be able to work more efficiently and safely in almost every workplace in the nation. In addition, you will also be able to give better customer service by building stronger relationships with new Hispanic customers. And-there's another added benefit. You will raise your communication skills to a whole new level.

As an adult, learning a new language requires a certain mind-set. It takes time, patience, and more than a little stubbornness. Just think about it. You didn't learn English over night- so you can't expect to know everything about Spanish by studying only a few weeks. Adults learn languages quite differently than children do. But- you will still make progress quickly by learning practical words and phrases first.

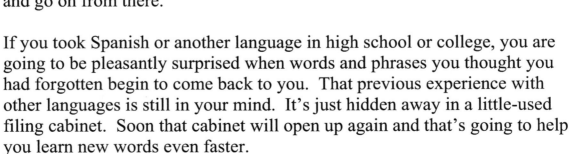

The secret to learning Spanish is having ***self-confidence and a great sense of humor***. To build self-confidence, you must first realize that the entire learning experience is painless and fun. Naturally, you are going to make mistakes. All of us make mistakes in English! So get ready to laugh, learn, and go on from there.

If you took Spanish or another language in high school or college, you are going to be pleasantly surprised when words and phrases you thought you had forgotten begin to come back to you. That previous experience with other languages is still in your mind. It's just hidden away in a little-used filing cabinet. Soon that cabinet will open up again and that's going to help you learn new words even faster.

But there's another idea you should consider too. What they told you in the traditional foreign language classroom was not exactly correct. There's no such thing as "*perfect Spanish*," just as there is no "*perfect English*." This leaves the door for good communication wide open!

*Español* is one of the world's most beautiful and expressive languages. Consider these other important facts as you begin:

- ✓ English and Spanish share a common Latin heritage, so literally thousands of words in our two languages are either *similar* or *identical*.
- ✓ Your ability to communicate is the most important thing, so your grammar and pronunciation don't have to be "*perfect*" for you to be understood.
- ✓ Some very practical and common expressions in Spanish can be communicated with a few simple words.
- ✓ As the number of Latinos in the United States increases, so do your opportunities to practice. Trying to say even a phrase or two in Spanish every day will help you learn faster.
- ✓ Relax! People who enjoy their learning experiences seem to acquire Spanish at a much faster pace than others.
- ✓ Set realistic goals and establish reasonable practice habits.
- ✓ When you speak even a little Spanish, you are showing a tremendous respect for Hispanic culture and people.
- ✓ Even a little Spanish or *poco español* goes a long way!

As you begin the process of learning Spanish, you are going to notice a few important differences. Speaking Spanish might feel and sound a little funny to you at first. Don't worry. This is a completely normal. It's because you are using muscles in your face that English doesn't require. Also, your inner ear is accustomed to hearing you speak English. People tell me it sounds and feels like Daffy Duck is inside your head! Just keep going! With practice and perseverance soon speaking and understanding Spanish will begin to feel more natural to you.

Many Americans know more Spanish than they realize- and pronounce it perfectly. Look at the list on page four and see how many Spanish words you recognize already. Taking the Spanish sounds you already know and practicing them will enable you to learn new principals of the Spanish language easier and faster. This is also a great way to help you build your confidence.

# Muchos Amigos

| Americano | Amigo | Hospital | Español | Doctor |
|---|---|---|---|---|
| Loco | Hotel | Oficina | Agua | Fiesta |
| Dinero | Señor | Señorita | Señora | Sombrero |
| Burrito | Taco | Olé | No problema | Accidente |
| Nachos | Salsa | Teléfono | Quesadilla | Margarita |
| Tequila | Tortilla | Bueno | Grande | Mucho |
| Blanco | Adiós | Gracias | Feliz Navidad | Hasta la vista. |
| Por favor | Pronto | Sí | Aplicación | Cinco de mayo |

# The Sounds of Spanish
## Información Básica

*No se preocupe.* One of your biggest concerns about acquiring a new language will be speaking well enough so that others can understand you. ***Don't worry!*** Spanish is close enough to English making a few mistakes along the way won't hurt your ability to communicate.

Here are the *five* vowel sounds in Spanish. These are the most important sounds in this language. Each vowel is pronounced the way it is written. Spanish vowels are never ***silent***. Even if there are two vowels together in a word, both of them will stand up and be heard.

| | | |
|---|---|---|
| A | (ah) | as in mama |
| E | (eh) | as in "hay or the "eh" in set |
| I | (ee) | as in deep |
| O | (oh) | as in open |
| U | (oo) | as in spoon |

Here are other sounds you'll need to remember.  Always pronounce them same way.  Spanish is a very consistent language.  The sounds the letters make don't shift around like they do in English.  Spanish is a very consistent language.

| *Spanish Letter* | | *English Sound* |
|---|---|---|
| **C** | (before an e or i) | s as in Sam: **cero: SAY**-row |
| **G** | (before an e or i) | h as in he: **energía:** n-air-**HE**-ah |
| **H** | | silent: **hacienda**: ah-see-**N**-da |
| **J** | | h as in hot: **Julio, HOO**-lee-oh |
| **LL** | | y as in yoyo: **tortilla**, tor-**TEE**-ya |
| **Ñ** | | ny as in canyon: **español**, ace-pan-**NYOL** |
| **QU** | | k as in kit: **tequila**, tay-**KEY**-la |
| **RR** | | The "rolled" r sound: **burro, BOO**-row |
| **V** | | v as in Victor: **Victor, VICK**-tor |
| **Z** | | s as in son: **Gonzales**, gone-**SA**-les |

***The Other Consonants*** - The remaining letters in Spanish are very similar to their equivalents in English.

## The Spanish Alphabet
### El alphabeto español

| A | ah | J | HO-ta | R | AIR-ray |
|---|---|---|---|---|---|
| **B** | bay | **K** | ka | **RR** | EH-rray |
| **C** | say | **L** | L-ay | **S** | S-ay |
| **CH** | chay | **LL** | A-yea | **T** | tay |
| **D** | day | **M** | M-ay | **U** | oo |
| **E** | A or EH | **N** | N-ay | **V** | vay |
| **F** | f-ay | **Ñ** | N-yea | **W** | DOE-blay-vay |
| **G** | hay | **O** | oh | **X** | 'a-kees |
| **H** | AH-chay | **P** | pay | **Y** | ee-gree-A-gah |
| **I** | ee | **Q** | coo | **Z** | SAY-ta |

# The Spanish Accent

In Spanish you will see two accent marks. Both are important and do different things. One of the diacritical marks you will notice is called a "tilde." It is only found over the letter "N." But, don't get the Ñ confused with N. The accent mark over Ñ makes it into a different letter entirely. In fact, it's one of four letters in the Spanish alphabet that the English alphabet doesn't have. The Ñ changes the sound of the letter to a combination of "ny." You'll hear the sound that this important letter makes in the English words "canyon" and "onion."

Occasionally you will see another accent mark over a letter in a Spanish word. The accent mark or "slash" mark shows you where to place vocal emphasis. So, when you see an accent mark over a letter in a Spanish word, just say that part of the word louder. For example: José (ho-**SAY**). These accented syllables are indicated in our pronunciation guides with bold, capital letters.

# Pronouncing Spanish Words

The pronunciation of Spanish words follows more regular rules than most other languages. That makes it easier to learn. Here are some tips to remember.

1. Most Spanish words that end with vowels are stressed or emphasized on the ***next to the last*** syllable.
2. Look for an accent mark. If the Spanish word has an accent in it, that's the emphasized syllable.
3. Words that end in consonants are stressed on the ***final*** syllable.

# Spanish Punctuation Marks

You will see two different punctuation marks in Spanish. First there's the upside down question mark (¿). You will see it at the beginning of all questions. It's there to simply let you know that what follows is a question and you will need to give your voice an upward inflection. It's the same inflection we use in English. Then, there's the upside down exclamation mark (¡). It's there to let you know that what follows should be vocally emphasized.

# Spanglish

In 1848 the treaty that ended the US-Mexican War signed over much of the Southwest to the United States. This transformed Spanish-speaking Mexicans into Americans overnight! Imagine waking up one morning and finding out you are a citizen of another country. As a result of the treaty, a new language was born that mixes the best of both worlds. Spanglish is a mixture of both our languages. Now, people who use Spanglish span generations, classes and nationalities. It's heard in pop music, seen in print, and used in conversations all through the Americas. Immigrants learning English may turn to Spanglish out of necessity and bilingual speakers use it because it's convenient. Even thought it's still frowned upon in most traditional language classes, it really is a great tool. Listed below are some of our *favoritos*.

| Truck/Trocka | Lunch/Lonche | No parking/No parque |
|:---:|:---:|:---:|
| Yard/Yarda | Break/Breaka | Cell Phone/El cel |

Some English words used as *Spanglish* are pronounced exactly as they are in English.

| El bar | El overtime |
|---|---|
| El break time | La party |
| El supermarket | La pizza |
| El closet | El record |
| La dishwasher | El rock-n-roll |
| El stress | El six-pack |

# Más Amigos

Using what you've learned about the sounds of Spanish, practice with these words. After you've pronounced everything on all three lists, go back through them again and mark the ones you can use on the job with a highlighter. Practice these words often.

## Easy Amigos

| | | |
|---|---|---|
| Aeropuerto | Flan | Padre |
| Aplicación | Flor | Paga |
| Accidente | Florería | Patata |
| Apartamento | Fruta | Persona |
| Avenida | General | Piña |
| Banana | Gimnasio | Plato |
| Banco | Hacienda | Policía |
| Bueno | Hamburguesa | Progreso |
| Café | Hasta mañana | Posible |
| Carro | Jamón | Rápido |
| Caución | Jalapeño | Restaurante |
| Centro | Identificación | Río |
| Conversación | Interesante | Rosbif |
| Chocolate | Importante | Servicio |
| Dentista | Leche | Super mercado |
| Diciembre | Macarrones | Supervisor |
| Dirección | Mesa | Té |
| Discusión | Mecánico | Teatro |
| Espárrago | Minuto | Televisión |
| Especial | Momento | Tomate |
| Familia | Motor | Tortilla |
| Fantástico | Nada | Vacación |
| Favorito | Nervioso | Valle |
| Final | Norte | Vino |

# Muchos Ways to Practicar

The more you listen to and use your *español* the easier it will be to learn it. There are lots of great ways to practice that won't cost your any money. Try these practice techniques for improving your skills:

- ✓ Next time you're at a Mexican restaurant, order your food in *español*.
- ✓ Start slowly. Practice one sound each week.
- ✓ Read Spanish language newspapers. They are usually free and easily available.
- ✓ Listen to Spanish language radio stations.
- ✓ Watch Spanish language television via satellite.
- ✓ Rent Spanish language videos, especially cartoons.
- ✓ Buy Spanish tapes and listen to them in the car while you commute.
- ✓ And speaking of tapes, there is such a variety of Latin *música* available, something will be right for you. Listening to music is a great way to train your ears to Spanish and have fun doing it. Personally, I like anything by Carlos Santana or the Salsa of Marc Anthony. What do you like?
- ✓ Visit Internet sites like *http://www.about.com*, where you can find all kinds of information about the Spanish language. They have a wonderful newsletter that comes to you free via e-mail. Most search engines, like Yahoo, have some sort of Spanish section.
- ✓ Next time you listen to a baseball game, keep track of all the Hispanic names you hear.
- ✓ Practice your Spanish every time the opportunity presents itself. This is the only way to get over your nervousness.
- ✓ Try to learn with a friend at work and practice together.

*What practice habits work for you?*
*Share them with us at:*
*info@speakeasyspanish.com*

# SpeakEasy's Tips and Techniques

**Remember**, when you're trying to communicate with a person who is "limited in English proficiency" or "LEP", *patience is a virtue*! Here are some easy things you can do to make the conversation easier for both of you. For more information on LEP visit this web site: www.lep.gov

✓ Speak slowly and distinctly.

✓ Do not use slang expressions or colorful terms.

✓ Get straight to the point! Unnecessary words cloud your meaning.

✓ Speak in a normal tone. Speaking *loudly* doesn't help anyone understand you any better!

✓ Look for cues to meaning in body language and facial expressions. Use gestures of your own to get your point across.

✓ You may not receive good eye contact.

✓ Latinos tend to stand closer to each other than North Americans do when they talk to each other, so your personal space could feel crowded. Stand your ground!

✓ Feel free to use gestures and body language of your own to communicate.

✓ Because of the way languages are learned, it is likely that the person you are talking to understands more of what you are saying, than he is able to verbalize. *So, be careful what you say!* No matter what the language, we always understand the bad words first!

# Beginning Words & Phrases

Well, let's get started!  In no time you will start gaining confidence.  Latinos will be delighted that you are trying to speak *español*.  Even if you can't remember a whole phrase, use the words you know.  Thank you *gracias* and please *por favor* go a long way toward establishing a rapport.

How many of these common words and phrases do you know?

| English | Español | Guide |
|---------|---------|-------|
| Hi! | ¡Hola! | **OH**-la |
| How are you? | ¿Cómo está? | **KO**-mo ace-**TA** |
| Fine | Muy bien. | mooy b-**N** |
| So so | Así así | ah-**SEE** ah-**SEE** |
| Bad | Mal | mal |
| Good morning | Buenos días | boo-**WAY**-nos **DEE**-ahs |
| Good afternoon | Buenas tardes | boo-**WAY**-nas **TAR**-days |
| Good night | Buenas noches. | boo-**WAY**-nas **NO**-chase |
| Sir or Mister | Señor | sen-**YOUR** |
| Mrs. or Ma'am | Señora | sen-**YOUR**-ah |
| Miss | Señorita | sen-your- **REE**-ta |
| What's your name? | ¿Cómo se llama? | **KO**-mo say **YA**-ma |
| My name is ___. | Me llamo ___. | may **YA**-mo |
| Nice to meet you. | ¡Mucho gusto! | **MOO**-cho **GOO**-stow |
| Thank you. | Gracias. | **GRA**-see-ahs |
| Please! | ¡Por favor! | pour-fa-**VOR** |
| You're welcome. | De nada.<br>Con mucho gusto | day **NA** da<br>con **MOO**-cho<br>**GOO**-stow |
| I'm sorry. | Lo siento. | low-see-**N**-toe |
| Excuse me. | ¡Perdón! | pear-**DON** |
| Bless you! | ¡Salud! | sah-**LEWD** |
| We'll see you! | ¡Hasta la vista | **AH**-sta la **VEE**-sta |
| Good-bye | Adiós | ah-dee-**OS** |

# Spanish Is Rápido – What Do I Do Now?

*Be honest!* One of the reasons you are hesitant to speak Spanish is that it sounds so fast! Naturally, you're afraid you won't understand. Here are some phrases that will help you. Make learning them a priority. *¿Comprende, amigo?*

| English | Español | Guide |
|---|---|---|
| I don't understand. | No comprendo. | no com-**PREN**-doe |
| Do you understand | ¿Comprende? | com-**PREN**-day |
| I speak a little Spanish. | Hablo poco español. | **AH**-blow **POE**-co ace-pan-**NYOL** |
| Do you speak English? | ¿Habla inglés? | **AH**-bla eng-**LACE** |
| Repeat, please. | Repita, por favor. | ray-**PETE**-ah pour fa-**VOR** |
| I'm studying Spanish. | Estudio español. | ace-**TOO**-dee-oh ace-pan-**NYOL** |
| Write it, please | Escribe, por favor | ace-**SCRE**-bay pour fa-**VOR** |
| Speak more slowly, please. | Habla más despacio, por favor. | **AH**-bla mas des-**PA**-see-oh pour fa-**VOR** |
| Thanks for your patience. | Gracias por su paciencia. | **GRA**-see-ahs pour sue pa-see-**N**-see-ah |
| How do you say it in Spanish? | ¿Como se dice en español? | **CO**-mo say **DEE**-say n ace-pan-**NYOL** |
| Where are you from? | ¿De dónde es? | day **DON**-day ace |
| May I help you? | ¿Puedo servirle? | pooh-**A**-doe seer-**VEER**-lay |

*The key here is <u>not</u> to pánico.*

Your Spanish-speaking employee or friend is having just as much trouble understanding you, as you are having understanding them! Hang in there! Between the two of you, *comunicación* will begin to take place.

# SpeakEasy's Conversaciones

| | |
|---|---|
| **USTED**: | Good morning, Sir. |
| **SR. GARCÍA** | Good morning.  How are you? |
| **USTED** | Fine, thanks. How are you? |
| **SR. GARCÍA** | OK, thanks. |

## Practice Conversation

¡Hola!

| | |
|---|---|
| **USTED** | May I help you?  My name is _____.  I speak a little Spanish.  What's your name? |
| **SRA. GARCÍA**: | My name is Carla García Hernandez.  I speak a little English. |
| **USTED** | Nice to meet you. |
| **SRA. GARCÍA** | Yes, nice to meet you. |

## Can you give the following information?

- ✓ Good morning or hi
- ✓ My name is _____.
- ✓ I speak a little Spanish.
- ✓ Do you speak English?
- ✓ Slower, please. Thank you.

# ¿Cuál Es Su Nombre Completo?

# Hispanic Names Have Four Parts

| First Name | Middle Name | Father's Surname | Mother's Surname |
|---|---|---|---|
| Primer Nombre | Segundo Nombre | Apellido Paterno | Apellido Materno |
| Carlos | Jesús | Santana | Rodríguez |
| José | Pedro | Cuervo | Álvarez |
| Poncho | Luis | Villa | García |
| Carmen | Elena | Miranda | Rivera |

**Start with**:  Señor,  Señora,  or  Señorita

## Use Both Names Or Only The Father's Last Name

Sr. Santana                              Sr. Cuervo
Sr. Villa                                   Sra. Miranda

## When a Woman Marries

She Keeps Her Father's Apellido Paterno
She Drops Her Apellido Materno
Last Is Her Husband's Apellido Paterno
Ask for her "Apellido Paterno de Esposo"

## Children Have The Apellido Paterno of Both Father and Mother

*If Carlos Santana married Carmen Miranda,
what is the Nombre Completo of the bebé*

**José Carlos ????  ?????**

# Spanish Nouns

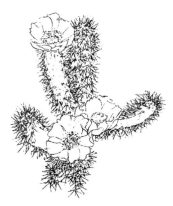

*Can words really have a gender?*

¡Si! Spanish belongs to the "romance" language family. It doesn't have anything to do with love, but it has a lot to do with the Romans. Because it evolved from Latin, Spanish words are grouped in two categories: masculine or feminine. Usually, the words were grouped by how they sounded, not by what they meant. Most of them follow regular rules, but there will always be a few exceptions!

Masculine words usually end with the letter "O".
Feminine words usually end with the letter "A".

El, la, los and las all mean "the." Look for them as clues to tell you a word's category.

| | |
|---|---|
| **El** | El niño, El muchacho |
| **Los** | Los niños, Los muchachos |
| **La** | La niña, La muchacha |
| **Las** | Las niñas, Las muchachas |

Most descriptive words will come after nouns in Spanish.

Descriptive words match the noun by gender and number.
La casa bonita or las casas bonitas

## Tips & Tidbits
Always remember that learning the *word* is the most important thing not learning the gender! That can wait. Concentrate on learning the words you need to know first!

# The Essentials of Spanish Verbs

- There are 3 types of verbs
  - ✓ **AR** - Hablar – to speak
  - ✓ **ER** - Comprender – to understand
  - ✓ **IR** - Vivir – to live

- When you want to say I speak, I understand, or I live, change the last two letters to an "O".
  - ✓ Hablo
  - ✓ Comprendo
  - ✓ Vivo

- When asking a question, such as do you speak, do you understand, or do you live, change the ending to an "A" or an "E".
  - ✓ Habla
  - ✓ Comprende
  - ✓ Vive

- To make a sentence negative, simply put "no" in front of the verb.
  - ✓ No hablo
  - ✓ No comprendo
  - ✓ No vivo

# ¡Acción!

There are so many English friendly *acción* words in the Spanish "AR" verb family. Many of them bear a strong resemblance to English verbs- and most of them share a simple, regular nature. They are a very important asset in on-the-job communication. We picked a few of our favorites to get you started. Look closely at the list on page 18. On it, you will recognize many comforting similarities between our languages that are practical too! Changing one letter will really expand your conversational skills.

In on-the-job conversations, people tend to use "I" and "you" to start many sentences. Of all the pronouns, these two are the most powerful and will work the hardest *for* you. So, that's where we'll start.

Here's an important difference between our languages. In English, the use of pronouns is essential because most of our verbs end the same way. For example, with I speak and you speak; speak remains the same. Our pronouns make all the difference. This isn't true in Spanish. Spanish-speaking people are listening for the letter on the end of the verb. That's what indicates who or what is being talked about. In most cases, you might not hear a pronoun. That's another reason that Spanish might sound a little fast to you: A whole series of words that are important in English are routinely eliminated in Spanish!

*Try this*: Treat the verbs in the "AR" family like you would *"to speak"* or *"hablar."* End the verb with an *O* when you're talking about yourself *"hablo"* or *"I speak"*. Change the verb ending from an "o" to an *A* for *"habla"* or *"you speak."* Use this form when you're talking to someone else.

| English | Español | Guide |
|---------|---------|-------|
| I need | Necesito | nay-say-**SEE**-toe |
| You need | Necesita | nay-say-**SEE**-ta |

**Note: To make a sentence negative, say no in front of the verb. No necesito. No necesita.

# The Sweet 16 Verbs

| English | Español | Guide |
|---|---|---|
| 1. To need | Necesitar | nay-say-see-**TAR** |
| 2. To use | Usar | oo-**SAR** |
| 3. To prepare | Preparar | pray-pa-**RAR** |
| 4. To accept | Aceptar | ah-sep-**TAR** |
| 5. To work | Trabajar | tra-baa-**HAR** |
| 6. To analyze | Analizar | ah-nal-lee-**SAR** |
| 7. To call | Llamar | ya-**MAR** |
| 8. To observe | Observar | ob-ser-**VAR** |
| 9. To insult | Insultar | een-sool-**TAR** |
| 10. To ask | Preguntar | prey-goon-**TAR** |
| 11. To carry | Llevar | yea-**VAR** |
| 12. To evacuate | Evacuar | a-vah-coo-**ARE** |
| 13. To cooperate | Cooperar | co-op-air-**RAR** |
| 14. To inform | Informar | een-for-**MAR** |
| 15. To pay | Pagar | pa-**GAR** |
| 16. To return | Regresar | ray-grey-**SAR** |

**The "Sweet 16 Verbs" were suggested by participants in SpeakEasy Spanish programs.

*Which verbs in the Sweet 16 do you use most often?  List your top six:*

1. _____

2. _____

3. _____

4. _____

5. _____

6. _____

*Now take your top six and by adding no, make a negative sentence:*

1. _____
2. _____
3. _____
4. _____
5. _____
6. _____

*Which verbs would you like to see on the list?  Write them below:*

1. _____
2. _____
3. _____
4. _____
5. _____
6. _____

## Study Tip

On your journey to Spanish proficiency, make prioritizing your vocabulary your ***número uno prioridad***!  Go through the "sweet 16" verb list in the table above with different colors of markers.  Highlight your "A" list in your favorite color.  Look at the vocabulary that remains.  Go through it again with a different color- one you don't like so much, and make it your "B" list. Don't begin on your "B" list until you are comfortable with your first choices.

## Scenarios

*Use verbs from the Sweet 16 to say the following:*

1. Use _____

2. Don't use _____

3. Prepare _____

4. I need *(Remember: Pronouns are often eliminated in Spanish)*

   _____

5. Evacuate _____

6. To inform_____

7. I observe _____

8. You observe _____

9. I pay _____

10. I don't pay _____

¡Necesito una breaka!

# The Big Five - Los Cinco Grandes

Now that you have had the opportunity to learn about the tremendous number of verbs that follow regular patterns in Spanish, it's time to take a look at others that don't follow the rules. They are unpredictable, but they are very important. In fact, they reflect some of man's oldest concepts. That's why they tend to be irregular. These words were in use long before language rules and patterns were set. So, here they are: to be (2), to have, to make, and to go. Because they don't follow the rules, you will need to memorize them, but that should be easy because you will use and hear them often.

In Spanish there are two verbs that mean *"to be"*. In English, that's I am, you are, he is, etc. The Spanish version is **ser** and **estar**. **Ser** is used to express permanent things like your nationality or profession. **Estar** is used when talking about location or conditions that change like a person's health.

| **Ser** | | **Estar** | |
|---|---|---|---|
| Yo **soy** | Nosotros **somos** | Yo **estoy** | Nosotros **estamos** |
| Tú **eres** | | Tú **estás** | |
| Él **es** | Ellos **son** | Él **está** | Ellos **están** |
| Ella **es** | Ellas **son** | Ella **está** | Ellas **están** |
| Usted **es** | Ustedes **son** | Usted **está** | Ustedes **están** |

The verb *"to have"* in Spanish is *muy importante*. In English we say that we are hot, cold, hungry, thirsty, right, wrong or sleepy, but in Spanish those are conditions that you have. Some of those expressions mean something totally different than you expected if you get the verbs confused, so be careful!

| **Tener** | |
|---|---|
| Yo **tengo** | Nosotros **tenemos** |
| Tú **tienes** | |
| Él **tiene** | Ellos **tienen** |
| Ella **tiene** | Ellas **tienen** |
| Usted **tiene** | Ustedes **tienen** |

In Spanish the verb that means, *"to do"* also means, *"to make."* It's not unusual for one verb to have multiple meanings. There are many expressions that require the use of this verb, but you will use it most when you talk about the weather. That's a safe subject and one that everyone, the world over, discusses! **¿Qué tiempo hace?** What's the weather? **Hace frío.** (It's cold.) **Hace sol.** (It's sunny). **Hace calor.** (It's hot) **Hace viento** (It's windy.). Here's two exceptions: **Está lloviendo.** (It's raining.) and **Está nevando.** (It's snowing.)

**Hacer**
| | |
|---|---|
| Yo **hago** | Nosotros **hacemos** |
| Tú **haces** | |
| Él **hace** | Ellos **hacen** |
| Ella **hace** | Ellas **hacen** |
| Usted **hace** | Ustedes **hacen**. |

The last of the big five is perhaps the easiest to use. It's the verb that means, *"to go"*. In Spanish, that's **ir**. It's pronounced like the English word ear. Both in English and in Spanish, we use parts of it to make the future tense, in other words, to talk about things that we are going to do. Look at the parts of ir. Then look back at the parts of the verb ser. Do you notice any similarities?

**Ir**
| | |
|---|---|
| Yo **voy** | Nosotros **vamos** |
| Tú **vas** | |
| Él **va** | Ellos **van** |
| Ella **va** | Ellas **van** |
| Usted **va** | Ustedes **van** |

When you want to say something that you are going to do, start with I'm going or voy. Next, insert the word "a" and the basic verb that states what it is that you're going to do. Try it! It's easy. Here are some examples.

| | |
|---|---|
| Voy a visitar a mi familia. | I am going to visit my family. |
| Voy a organizar los trabajadores. | I am going to organize the workers. |
| Mario va a comprar las plantas. | Mario is going to buy the plants. |

***The whole concept of irregular verbs is can be quite daunting. Don't let it defeat you! We have many verbs like this in English. In fact, every language has them. The only way to master them is to practice by using them. Make them your own! Try writing different parts of a verb on your desk calendar. That way, it will be there in front of you every time you look down. When you see it, say it to yourself. Then, you'll have it conquered in no time.

## What's the Weather? - ¿Qué tiempo hace?

No matter what the culture is, a general topic for discussion is always the weather. If you're traveling, most of your plans will be contingent upon it. Discussing the weather in Spanish requires a different verb from the one we use in English. It's one of the big five. The Spanish use the verb *hacer* (to do or to make) to describe the weather.

| Phrase | Translation |
| --- | --- |
| Hace buen tiempo | To be nice weather |
| Hace calor | To be hot |
| Hace fresco | To be cool |
| Hace sol | To be sunny |
| Hace viento | To be windy |
| Hace frío | To be cold |
| Lluvia | Rain |
| Llover | To rain |
| ¿Qué tiempo hace? | What's the weather? |

*Note: In America we use the Fahrenheit scale for measuring the temperature. Latin Americans use the Celsius scale. What is the difference?*

## Season: Estación
Spring: Primavera          Summer: Verano
Autumn: Otoño              Winter: Invierno

# Descriptions or Descripciones

Describing things in Spanish can present problems for English speakers. There are three reasons why this gives us trouble. First, there is the location of the adjective. In English, descriptive words go in front of the noun like white cat, for example. In Spanish, the noun is the most important element, so it comes first (***gato blanco***). However, it gets a little more complicated because there are a few adjectives that are placed before the noun- and they are very common: For example: large or ***grande*** (***grande gato blanco***). Next, since Spanish nouns are divided into masculine and feminine categories, the descriptive word should match it by category and by number (singular or plural). This leads us to challenge number three: changing the spelling of the adjective. You might need to change a final "o" to an "a" to change the category. Here is a list of descriptive words that can be used in almost any profession.

| English | Español | English | Español |
|---------|---------|---------|---------|
| **Alive** | Vivo | **Dead** | Muerto |
| **Good** | Bueno | **Bad** | Malo |
| **Better** | Mejor | **Worse** | Peor |
| **Big** | Grande | **Small** | Pequeño |
| **Clean** | Limpio | **Dirty** | Sucio |
| **Hot** | Caliente | **Cold** | Frío |
| **Sane** | Cuerdo | **Crazy** | Loco |
| **Safe** | Seguro | **Dangerous** | Peligroso |
| **Easy** | Fácil | **Difficult** | Difícil |
| **Full** | Lleno | **Empty** | Vacío |
| **Fast** | Rápido | **Slow** | Lento |
| **Hard** | Duro | **Soft** | Blando |
| **New** | Nuevo | **Old** | Viejo |
| **Rich** | Rico | **Poor** | Pobre |
| **Pretty** | Bonito | **Ugly** | Feo |
| **Quiet** | Tranquilo | **Restless** | Inquieto |
| **Tall** | Alto | **Short** | Bajo |
| **Well** | Bien | **Sick** | Enfermo |
| **Strong** | Fuerte | **Weak** | Débil |

# How Much - ¿Cuánto?

| Number | Español | Pronunciation Guide |
|--------|---------|---------------------|
| 0 | Cero | **SAY**-row |
| 1 | Uno | **OO**-no |
| 2 | Dos | dose |
| 3 | Tres | trays |
| 4 | Cuatro | coo-**AH**-trow |
| 5 | Cinco | **SINK**-oh |
| 6 | Seis | **SAY**-ees |
| 7 | Siete | see-**A**-tay |
| 8 | Ocho | **OH**-cho |
| 9 | Nueve | new-**A**-vay |
| 10 | Diez | dee-**ACE** |
| 11 | Once | **ON**-say |
| 12 | Doce | **DOSE**-a |
| 13 | Trece | **TRAY**-say |
| 14 | Catorce | ca-**TOR**-say |
| 15 | Quince | **KEEN**-say |
| 16 | Diez y seis | dee-**ACE**-e-**SAY**-ees |
| 17 | Diez y siete | dee-**ACE**-e-see-**ATE**-tay |
| 18 | Diez y ocho | dee-**ACE**-e-**OH**-cho |
| 19 | Diez y nueve | dee-**ACE**-e-new-**A**-vay |
| 20 | Veinte | **VAIN**-tay |
| 21 | Veinte y uno | **VAIN**-tay e **OO**-no |
| 22 | Veinte y dos | **VAIN**-tay e dose |
| 23 | Veinte y tres | **VAIN**-tay e trays |
| 24 | Veinte y cuatro | **VAIN**-tay e coo-**AH**-trow |
| 25 | Veinte y cinco | **VAIN**-tay e **SINK**-oh |
| 26 | Veinte y seis | **VAIN**-tay e **SAY**-ees |
| 27 | Veinte y siete | **VAIN**-tay e see-**A**-tay |
| 28 | Veinte y ocho | **VAIN**-tay e **OH**-cho |
| 29 | Veinte y nueve | **VAIN**-tay e new-**A**-vay |
| 30 | Treinta | **TRAIN**-ta |
| 40 | Cuarenta | kwah-**RAIN**-ta |
| 50 | Cincuenta | seen-**KWAIN**-ta |
| 60 | Sesenta | say-**SAIN**-ta |
| 70 | Setenta | say-**TAIN**-ta |
| 80 | Ochenta | oh-**CHAIN**-ta |
| 90 | Noventa | no-**VAIN**-ta |
| 100 | Cien | see-**IN** |
| 200 | Doscientos | dose-see-**N**-toes |
| 300 | Trescientos | tray-see-**N**-toes |
| 400 | Cuatrocientos | coo-**AH**-troh-see-**N**-toes |
| 500 | Quinientos | keen-e-**N**-toes |
| 600 | Seiscientos | **SAY**-ees-see-**N**-toes |
| 700 | Setecientos | **SAY**-tay-see-**N**-toes |
| 800 | Ochocientos | **OH**-choh-see-**N**-toes |
| 900 | Novecientos | **NO**-vay-see-**N**-toes |
| 1,000 | Mil | meal |

# Los Días de la Semana y los Meses del Año
## Los Días de la Semana

| English | Español | Guide |
|---------|---------|-------|
| Monday | Lunes | **LOON**-ace |
| Tuesday | Martes | **MAR**-tays |
| Wednesday | Miércoles | me-**AIR**-co-lace |
| Thursday | Jueves | who-**WAVE**-ace |
| Friday | Viernes | vee-**YAIR**-nace |
| Saturday | Sábado | **SAH**-ba-doe |
| Sunday | Domingo | doe-**MING**-go |

*It's important to remember when expressing a date in Spanish give the number of the day first followed by the month. Use this format:*
*El (date) de (month).*

## Los Meses del Año

| English | Español | Guide |
|---------|---------|-------|
| January | Enero | n-**NAY**-row |
| February | Febrero | fay-**BRAY**-row |
| March | Marzo | **MAR**-so |
| April | Abril | ah-**BRILL** |
| May | Mayo | **MY**-oh |
| June | Junio | **WHO**-knee-oh |
| July | Julio | **WHO**-lee-oh |
| August | Agosto | ah-**GOSE**-toe |
| September | Septiembre | sep-tee-**EM**-bray |
| October | Octubre | oc-**TOO**-bray |
| November | Noviembre | no-vee-**EM**-bray |
| December | Diciembre | dee-see-**EM**-bray |

Your job starts (*day of the week*) el (*number*) de (*month*).
*Su empleo comienza lunes, el 11 de octubre.*

Your appointment is Monday the 5th of May.
*Su cita es lunes el cinco de mayo.*

# Practicing Numbers & Dates

*Practice these important items by using numbers, days of the week, and months of the year:*

✓ Your social security number

✓ Your driver's license number

✓ The numbers in your address

✓ Your zip code

✓ Your phone number

✓ Your birth date

✓ Your children's birth dates

✓ The dates of holidays

✓ License tags of the cars in front of you, when you are stopped in

traffic. Combine the Spanish alphabet with this exercise.

✓ Phone numbers you see on billboards

✓ Numbers found on street signs

✓ Phone numbers when you dial them at work or at home

✓ The appointments on your personal calendar

✓ Your wedding anniversary

✓ The dates of all your Spanish classes

# ¿Qué Hora Es?
## What Time Is It?

The concept of time is something that varies from culture to culture. Many countries put less emphasis on being on time than Americans do. For Latinos working in America, this is rapidly changing. They quickly learn the value of **puntualidad. Es importante!**

Learning to tell time is another good way to put your numbers in Spanish to good use . **¿Qué hora es?** means **what time is it?**

| | |
|---|---|
| **It's one o'clock.** | **Es la una.** |
| **It's two o'clock.** | **Son las dos.** |
| **It's 3:30.** | **Son las tres y media.** |
| **It's 5:45.** | **Son las seis menos quince.** |

Use the phrases **de la mañana** to indicate morning and **de la tarde** to indicate afternoon. Also midnight is **medianoche**. Noon is **mediodía**.

To find out at what time something takes place ask:   **¿A qué hora…?**

| | |
|---|---|
| **¿A qué hora es la reunión?** | **What time is the meeting?** |
| **¿A qué hora termina?** | **What time do you finish?** |

Spanish speakers sometimes use the 24-hour clock for departures and arrivals of trains and flights, etc.
las doce cero cinco
las diez y siete cincuenta y dos
las veinte y tres diez
las siete quince

## Para practicar

1. Using the word for meeting, la reunion, say that the meeting takes place on the hour throughout your regular workday. **La reunión es a las ocho.**
2. Tell Sr. Rojas what time your store opens and closes.
3. Using the days of the week and the time to explain a work schedule. Your work schedule is…. **Su horario es…..**

# The Questions Everyone Should Know

| English | Español | Guide |
|---|---|---|
| Who? | ¿Quién? | key-**N** |
| Whose? | ¿De quién? | day key-**N** |
| What? | ¿Qué? | kay |
| Which? | ¿Cuál? | coo-**ALL** |
| When? | ¿Cuándo? | **KWAN**-doe |
| Where? | ¿Dónde? | **DON**-day |
| Why? | ¿Por qué? | pour **KAY** |
| How? | ¿Cómo? | **CO**-mo |
| What's happening? | ¿Qué pasa? | kay **PA**-sa |
| What happened? | ¿Qué pasó? | kay pa-**SO** |
| How much? | ¿Cuánto? | **KWAN**-toe |
| How many | ¿Cuántos? | **KWAN**-toes |

When you ask a question in Spanish, it will take on the same form as a question does in English. Start with the question word that asks the information you need. Follow the question word with a verb, and give your voice an upward inflection.

In Spanish you can also make a question by ending your sentence with ¿no? Here's an example: Cancún está en México, ¿no? When you end a sentence with "no" like this, it takes on the meaning of "isn't it."

## The Most Common Questions

How are you?                    ¿Cómo está?
How much does it cost?          ¿Cuánto cuesta?
Where are you from?             ¿De dónde es?

Did you notice the upside down question mark (¿) at the beginning of each question? All questions in Spanish begin with this punctuation mark. All exclamatory phrases like, Hi! Begin with an upside down exclamation point like this: ¡Hola! You can do this on your word processor. Refer to "Typing in Spanish with Microsoft Word" in your table of contents for details.

# Getting the Información
## La entrevista – The Interview

Listed below are the most common questions used during an interview. It's not always necessary to make a complete sentence to have good communication. The information you are asking for is much more important than the phrase "what is your"? As long as you remember to make what you say *sound* like a question by giving your voice an *upward* inflection, people will interpret what you've said *as* a question. Using the form on the following page, work with a partner to practice giving and receiving information. Make up new answers about yourself for each practice session. You will always be asking the same questions, but the answers you get will always be different!

**What's your. . .**          **¿Cuál es su. . .**
                          *Coo-ALL ace sue*

| English | Español |
|---|---|
| Full name | Nombre completo |
| First name | Primer nombre |
| Last name | Apellido |
| Paternal surname | Apellido paterno |
| Maternal surname | Apellido materno |
| Address | Dirección |
| Apartment number | Número de  apartamento |
| Age | Edad |
| Date of birth | Fecha de nacimiento |
| Nationality | Nacionalidad |
| Place of birth | Lugar de nacimiento |
| Place of employment | Lugar de empleo |
| Occupation | Ocupación |
| Home telephone number | Número de teléfono de su casa |
| Work telephone number | Número de teléfono de su empleo |
| Marital status | Estado civil |
| Driver's license number | Número de licencia |
| Social security number | Número de seguro social |

# Información Básica
## Imprima por favor

Fecha: _____
                           Mes      Día      Año

**Sr.**
**Sra.**
**Srta.**_____
        *Primer Nombre      Segundo Nombre      Apellido Paterno      Apellido Materno (Esposo)*

**Dirección:**_____
                                    *Calle*

_____
*Ciudad*                          *Estado*                    *Zona postal*

**Teléfono:** Casa _____      Empleo_____

               Cel_____      Fax _____

**Correo electrónico** _____

**Número de seguro social:** _____-_____-_____

**Número de identificación de contribuyente (TIN):**_____

**Fecha de nacimiento** _____
                         Mes        Día        Año

**Número de la licencia:** _____

**Ocupación:** _____

**Lugar de empleo**_____

**Estado civil:**   ☐   Casado (a)
                    ☐   Soltero (a)
                    ☐   Divorciado (a)
                    ☐   Separado (a)
                    ☐   Viudo (a)

**Nombre de esposo:**_____
                     *Primer Nombre      Segundo Nombre   Apellido Paterno      Apellido Materno*
**Nombre de esposa:** _____
                     *Primer Nombre      Segundo Nombre   Apellido Paterno      Apellido Materno/Esposo*

**En caso de emergencia:**_____**Teléfono:** _____

**Firma:** _____      **Fecha:** _____

# The Family - La Familia

Family values are extremely important to Latinos. This is something all of us have in common. Many Latinos have left their families in their native countries to come here for economic reasons. No sacrifice is too great for *la familia*.

Children are considered to be precious gifts. Wives, mothers and grandmothers are greatly respected. Remember that all Hispanics have their mother's surname or *materno apellido*. You are going to hear members of the family from your Hispanic customers. It's something all of us like to talk about!

| English | Español | Guide |
|---|---|---|
| Aunt | Tía | **TEE**-ah |
| Brother | Hermano | air-**MAN**-oh |
| Brother-in-law | Cuñado | coon-**YA**-doe |
| Child | Niño, niña | **KNEE**-nyo, **KNEE**-nya |
| Cousin | Primo, prima | **PRE**-mo, **PRE**-ma |
| Daughter | Hija | **E**-ha |
| Daughter-in-law | Nuera | new-**AIR**-rah |
| Father | Padre | **PA**-dray |
| Father-in-law | Suegro | soo-**A**-grow |
| Granddaughter | Nieta | knee-**A**-tah |
| Grandfather | Abuelo | ah-boo-**A**-low |
| Grandmother | Abuela | ah-boo-**A**-la |
| Grandson | Nieto | knee-**A**-toe |
| Husband | Esposo | ace-**PO**-so |
| Mother | Madre | **MA**-dray |
| Mother-in-law | Suegra | soo-**A**-gra |
| Sister | Hermana | air-**MAN**-ah |
| Sister-in-law | Cuñada | coon-**YA**-da |
| Son | Hijo | **E**-ho |
| Son-in-law | Yerno | **YEAIR**-no |
| Teenager | Muchacho, muchacha | moo-**CHA**-cho, moo-**CHA**-cha |

| English | Español | Guide |
|---------|---------|-------|
| Uncle | Tío | **TEE**-oh |
| Wife | Esposa | ace-**POE**-sa |
| Boyfriend/Girlfriend | Novio, Novia | **NO**-v-oh  **NO**-v-ah |

## Para Practicar

Using the verb *tener* (to have), tell your practice partner how many relatives you have in your family.  Start like this: *Tengo* or I have.  Follow that with the number and the member of the family that you are talking about.  You will find more about *tener* in the next chapter.  Even though it isn't a regular verb, it's very practical.  You will use it in many different ways.

## En mi familia…..

1. I have two sons. _____

2. I have three daughters. _____

3. My son's name is _____

4. My (Mi) daughter's name is _____

5. My wife's name is _____

6. I have three uncles. _____

7. I have four aunts. _____

8. I have no brothers. _____

9. I have one (una) sister. _____

10. I have two brothers-in-law. _____

# Meals & Beverages

As you learn the names of meals, beverages, and foods, here's a tip on how to start the process. Review the words in each list. Then, highlight the ones that you are most likely to use. *Always* learn the words that you are going to use first. It's only natural. If you don't like decaffeinated coffee, you aren't likely to use that term. So make *your* list practical for what *you* need. That's the SpeakEasy way!

| English | Español | Guide |
|---|---|---|
| Meal | Comida | co-**ME**-da |
| Appetizer | Tapas | **TA**-pas |
| Breakfast | Desayuno | day-say-**UNO** |
| Lunch | Almuerzo | al-moo-**AIR**-so |
| Dinner | Cena | **SAY**-na |
| Dessert | Postre | **POS**-tray |
| Beer | Cerveza | ser-**VAY**-sa |
| Coffee | Café | ca-**FAY** |
| Decaffeinated coffee | Café descafeinado | ca-**FAY** des-ca-fay-**NA**-doe |
| Diet soda | Refresco dieta | ray-**FRAYS**-co d-**EH**-ta |
| Ice | Hielo | ee-**A**-low |
| Iced tea | Té helado | tay a-**LA**-doe |
| Juice | Jugo | **WHO**-go |
| Lemonade | Limonada | lee-mon-**NA**-da |
| Milkshake | Batido | ba-**TEE**-doe |
| Red wine | Vino tinto | **V**-no **TEEN**-toe |
| Salad | Ensalada | n-sa-**LA**-da |
| Sandwich | Sándwich | sandwich |
| Snack | Merienda | may-ree-**N**-da |
| Soft drink | Refresco Soda | ray-**FRES**-co **SO**-da |
| Soup | Sopa | **SO**-pa |
| Tea | Té | tay |
| Water | Agua | **AH**-goo-ah |
| White wine | Vino blanco | **V**-no **BLAN**-co |
| Wine | Vino | **V**-no |

# Meats & Seafood

Foods are always fun to learn and practice. After you've gone through the lists of various food types and highlighted your favorites, break down the work even more by making a list of your favorite breakfast, lunch, and dinner foods. Then, make a list of your favorite snacks and beverages. You can breakdown the vocabulary even farther if you make a list of the foods and beverages that you dislike, too. Next put your lists on index cards. Now you're ready to order anywhere you need to use *español*. Make sure to take your cards with you when you travel. This is a great way to build practice time into an already busy day!

| English | Español | Guide |
|---------|---------|-------|
| Meat | Carne | **CAR**-nay |
| Rare | Poco cocida | **PO**-co co-**SEE**-da |
| Medium | Medio cocida | **MAY**-d-oh co-**SEE**-da |
| Well-done | Bien cocida | b-**N** co-**SEE**-da |
| Bacon | Tocino | to-**SEE**-no |
| Beef | Carne de vaca | **CAR**-nay day **VA**-ca |
| Broth | Caldo | **CAL**-doe |
| Chicken | Pollo | **POE**-yo |
| Clam | Almeja | al-**MAY**-ha |
| Crab | Cangrejo | can-**GREY**-ho |
| Fish | Pescado | pace-**KA**-doe |
| Ground beef | Carne molida | **CAR**-nay mo-**LEE**-da |
| Ham | Jamón | ha-**MON** |
| Hamburger | Hamburguesa | am-burr-**GAY**-sa |
| Hot Dog | Perro caliente | **PAY**-row ca-lee-**N**-tay |
| Lamb | Cordero | cor-**DAY**-row |
| Liver | Hígado | **E**-ga-doe |
| Lobster | Langosta | lan-**GO**-sta |
| Meatball | Albóndiga | al-**BONE**-dee-ga |
| Oyster | Ostra | **OH**-stra |
| Pork | Cerdo | **SER**-doe |

| English | Español | Guide |
|---------|---------|-------|
| Pork chop | Chuleta de puerco | chew-**LAY**-ta day poo-**AIR**-co |
| Poultry | Carne de ave | **CAR**-nay day **AH**-vay |
| Roast beef | Rosbif | ros-**BEEF** |
| Sausage | Salchicha | sal-**CHI**-cha |
| Scallops | Vieira | ve-a-**E**-rah |
| Seafood | Mariscos | ma-**REES**-cos |
| Shrimp | Camarón | ca-ma-**RON** |
| Steak | Bistec | **BEE**-stek |
| Stew | Guiso | goo-**E**-so |
| Tuna | Atún | ah-**TOON** |
| Turkey | Pavo | **PA**-vo |
| Veal | Ternera | ter-**NAY**-rah |

## Para Practicar:

1. List five of your favorite meats: _____

   _____

2. How do you like your steak to be prepared: _____

3. List three of your favorite seafoods: _____

   _____

4. List meats that you do not like or have never tried: _____

   _____

5. List all the poultry: _____

   _____

6. Which meats could you order at fast-food restaurants? _____

   _____

7. Which meats are pork products? _____

# Fruits

Hispanic tastes in foods and beverages are influencing the items we see on supermarket shelves.  As a result, tropical fruit and vegetable varieties are much easier to find, and selections in the "ethnic" aisle are growing.  A recent on-line study of the Hispanic population's taste preferences in beverages and sweets found that a high percentage preferred fruit flavors.  Latinos tend to enjoy fruit-flavored sodas over colas.  Here is a list of the most popular fruit flavors:  Pineapple, mango, watermelon, strawberry, citrus and grape.  The next time you go shopping, visit the ethnic aisle in your market and pick up a fruit-flavored soda.  The flavor selection may surprise you.  Chances are you'll find these unusual beverages to be a refreshing change of pace!

| English | Español | Guide |
| --- | --- | --- |
| Fruit | Fruta | **FRU**-ta |
| Apple | Manzana | man-**SAN**-na |
| Apricot | Durazno | doo-**RAHS**-no |
| Banana | Plátano | **PLA**-ta-no |
| Blackberry | Mora | **MOW**-rah |
| Blueberry | Arándano | ah-**RAHN**-da-no |
| Cantaloupe | Melón<br>Cantalupo | may-**LOAN**<br>can-ta-**LOO**-poe |
| Cherry | Cereza | say-**RAY**-sa |
| Coconut | Coco | **CO**-co |
| Fig | Higo | **E**-go |
| Grape | Uva | **OO**-va |
| Grapefruit | Toronja | toe-**ROAN**-ha |
| Lemon | Limón | lee-**MON** |
| Lime | Lima | **LEE**-ma |
| Mango | Mango | **MAN**-go |
| Orange | Naranja | na-**RAN**-ha |
| Papaya | Papaya | pa-**PIE**-ya |
| Peach | Melocotón | may-low-co-**TON** |
| Pear | Pera | **PAY**-rah |
| Pineapple | Piña | **PEEN**-ya |
| Plum | Ciruela | see-roo-**A**-la |

| English | Español | Guide |
|---------|---------|-------|
| Prune | Ciruela pasa | see-roo-**A**-la **PA**-sa |
| Raisin | Pasita | pa-**SEE**-ta |
| Strawberry | Fresa | **FRAY**-sa |
| Tamarind | Tamarindo | ta-ma-**REEN**-doe |
| Watermelon | Sandía | san-**DEE**-ah |

## Para Practicar:

1. List your favorite fruits: _____
_____

2. List all the citrus fruits: _____
_____

3. List any fruits you've never tasted: _____
_____

4. Which fruits do you consider to be "tropical"? _____
_____

5. List four fruits that are associated with juice: _____
_____

6. Which fruits are melons? _____
_____

7. Name five fruits that make great pies: _____
_____

8. Name three fruits that make great ice-cream flavors: _____
_____

9. Name any fruits that you don't like: _____
_____

# Vegetables

Hispanic tastes in foods are as diverse as Hispanic people are. Each country in Latin America has its own traditional favorites. Often, these foods are quite different from what you might imagine. For example, Argentineans have a great reputation for liking steak, while many Chileans enjoy spaghetti, and everyone doesn't eat foods laced with hot chilies. Over all, Latin Americans tend to eat more fresh fruits and vegetables than other segments of the population. If you've never tried Latin American styles of cooking, look for your favorite vegetable from the list below and go on-line to search for a recipe. Better yet, pick a "veggie" you've never tried and prepare it. This is a super way to make learning come to life!

| English | Español | Guide |
|---------|---------|-------|
| **Vegetables** | **Vegetales** | vay-he-**TA**-lace |
| Artichoke | Alcachofa | al-ca-**CHO**-fa |
| Asparagus | Espárragos | ace-**PA**-rah-gos |
| Avocado | Aguacate | agua-**CA**-tay |
| Dried Beans | Frijoles | free-**HO**-lace |
| Beet | Betabel | bay-ta-**BELL** |
| Black beans | Frijoles negros | free-**HO**-lace **NAY**-grows |
| Broccoli | Brócoli | **BRO**-co-lee |
| Brussels sprouts | Col de Bruselas | col day brew-**SAY**-las |
| Cabbage | Col | col |
| Carrot | Zanahoria | sa-na-**OR**-ree-ah |
| Cauliflower | Coliflor | co-lee-**FLOOR** |
| Celery | Apio | **AH**-p-oh |
| Corn | Maíz | ma-**EES** |
| Corn on the cob | Elote | a-**LOW**-tay |
| Cucumber | Pepino | pay-**P**-no |
| Green bean | Ejote | a-**HOE**-tay |
| Green bell pepper | Pimiento verde | p-me-**N**-toe **VER**-day |
| Green peas | Guisantes | gee-**SAN**-tays |

| English | Español | Guide |
|---|---|---|
| Leek | Puerro | poo-**A**-row |
| Lettuce | Lechuga | lay-**CHEW**-ga |
| Mushroom | Champiñón | cham-peen-**YON** |
| Onion | Cebolla | say-**BOY**-ya |
| Pea | Guisante | goo-ee-**SAN**-tay |
| Pepper | Pimiento | p-me-**N**-toe |
| Potato | Patata | pa-**TA**-ta |
| Pumpkin | Calabaza | ca-la-**BA**-sa |
| Squash | Calabacera | ca-la-ba-**SER**-rah |
| Sweet potato | Camote | ca-**MO**-tay |
| Tomato | Tomate | to-**MA**-tay |
| Zucchini | Calabacita verde | ca-la-ba-**SEE**-ta **VER**-day |

## Para Practicar:

1. List your favorite vegetables: _____

_____

2. List your least favorite vegetables: _____

_____

3. Which vegetables could you invite to a barbecue? _____

_____

4. Which of the vegetables do you enjoy on a pizza? _____

_____

5. Which vegetables could you put in a stew? _____

_____

6. Which vegetables could you put in a salad? _____

_____

7. Name the different kinds of beans: _____

_____

# Dairy & Egg Products

Dairy products and eggs are dietary staples around the world. No matter where you travel or live, you'll be amazed at the variety of mouth-watering dishes that involve these two culinary giants. Both are great sources of protein, and literally the basis of millions of recipes. Two world-class Latin American dishes come to mind in this category: Tres Leches Cake and Huevos Rancheros.

Tres Leches Cake or "three milk cake" is exactly what the name describes. It's a rich, butter cake soaked in three different milks: sweetened condensed milk, evaporated milk and whole milk or heavy cream. Combining the three milks provides just the right sweetness and moistness. Some carry the milk theme even farther by serving Tres Leches Cake with a coconut milk or goat's milk and caramel sauce. What a way to end a memorable meal!

Huevos Rancheros means "rancher's eggs" or "ranch-styled" eggs, and there are many different ways to prepare it. Some recipes call for beans and cheese, but traditionally, the dish consists of fried eggs served on tortillas with a spicy tomato-chile salsa on the side. Huevos Rancheros got its name in Mexico where it was served as a second breakfast to ranch hands after they finished morning chores. Now, it's not just for breakfast anymore and can also be served for a quick brunch or supper.

| English | Español | Guide |
|---|---|---|
| Dairy Products | Productos Lácteos | pro-**DUKE**-toes **LACK**-tay-ohs |
| 2% milk | Leche de dos por ciento | **LAY**-che day dose pour see-**N**-toe |
| Butter | Mantequilla | man-tay-**KEY**-ya |
| Butter milk | Suero | sue-**A**-row |
| Cheese | Queso | **KAY**-so |
| Chocolate milk | Leche de chocolate | **LAY**-che day cho-ko-**LA**-tay |
| Cottage cheese | Requesón | ray-kay-**SEWN** |

| English | Español | Guide |
| --- | --- | --- |
| Cream | Crema | **CRAY**-ma |
| Cream cheese | Queso crema | **KAY**-so **CRAY**-ma |
| Egg | Huevo | oo-**WAVE**-oh |
| Egg white | Clara de huevo | **CLA**-rah day oo-**WAVE**-oh |
| Egg yolk | Yema de huevo | **YEA**-ma day oo-**WAVE**-oh |
| Evaporated milk | Leche evaporada | **LAY**-che a-vah-poor-**RAH**-da |
| Half and half | Leche con crema | **LAY**-che con **CRAY**-ma |
| Hard-boiled egg | Huevo duro | oo-**WAVE**-oh **DO**-row |
| Ice-cream | Helado | a-**LA**-doe |
| Margarine | Margarina | mar-gar-**E**-na |
| Milk | Leche | **LAY**-che |
| Non-fat milk | Leche sin grasa | **LAY**-che seen **GRA**-sa |
| Omelet | Tortilla de huevos | tor-**T**-ya day oo-**WAVE**-ohs |
| Parmesan cheese | Queso parmesano | **KAY**-so par-may-**SAN**-no |
| Scrambled egg | Huevo revuelto | oo-**WAVE**-oh ray-voo-**L**-toe |
| Soft boiled egg | Huevo pasado por agua | oo-**WAVE**-oh pa-**SA**-doe poor **AH**-goo-ah |
| Sour cream | Crema de leche agria | **CRAY**-ma day **LAY**-che ah-**GREE**-ah |
| Sunny-side up | Yema blanda | **YEA**-ma **BLAN**-da |
| Sweetened condensed milk | Leche condensada | **LAY**-che con-den-**SA**-da |
| Whole milk | Leche entera | **LAY**-che enn-**TAY**-rah |
| Yogurt | Yogurt | yo-**GOOR** |

# Bread, Pasta, Dessert and More

Breads, pastas and desserts are becoming more varied as Latin American cooking is influenced by other cultures. Every major city throughout the Americas will have at least one bakery featuring French bread or pizza dough, but flat breads, such as tortillas, are considered kitchen staples. Traditionally, they are made from corn, but wheat varieties also exist. Some restaurants and bakeries still make them by hand, the old-fashioned way. There's really nothing like the taste of a freshly grilled tortilla.

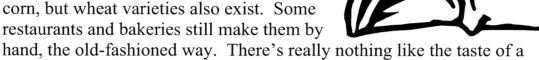

Chocolate is another important food with Latin American ties. It was discovered more than 2,000 years ago by ancient Mesoamericans in the tropical rainforests of the Americas. Aztecs and Mayans were among the first ancient peoples to use and enjoy chocolate. Chocolate was different in those days because it wasn't sweetened. Ground and mixed with other spices, it was made into a frothy, slightly bitter beverage. Legend has it that only Aztec kings, priests and decorated soldiers were allowed to drink this "hot chocolate." When the Spanish arrived in the Americas, they were introduced to the magical mixture and quickly took it back to Spain. Eventually, sugar and milk were added and the rest is history!

| English | Español | Guide |
|---------|---------|-------|
| Bread | Pan | pahn |
| Cake | Torta | **TOR**-ta |
| Candy | Dulce | **DOOL**-say |
| Cereal | Cereal | say-ray-**AL** |
| Chips | Tostaditas | tos-ta-**D**-tas |
| Chocolate | Chocolate | cho-co-**LA**-tay |
| Cookie | Galleta | ga-**YEA**-ta |
| Cracker | Galleta salada | ga-**YEA**-ta sa-**LA**-da |
| Cupcake | Pastelito | pas-tay-**LEE**-toe |
| Custard | Flan | flahn |
| Honey | Miel | mee-**L** |
| Ice cream | Helado | a-**LA**-doe |

| English | Español | Guide |
|---|---|---|
| Jam | Mermelada | mer-may-**LA**-da |
| Macaroni | Macarrones | ma-ca-**RONE**-ace |
| Noodles | Fideos | fe-**DAY**-ohs |
| Nut | Nuez | new-**ACE** |
| Oatmeal | Avena | ah-**VAY**-na |
| Pancakes | Panqueques | pan-**KAY**-kays |
| Pastry | Pastelería | pas-tell-lay-**REE**-ah |
| Peanut butter | Crema de cacahuate | **CRAY**-ma day ca-ca-who-**A**-tay |
| Pie | Pastel | pas-**TEL** |
| Pudding | Pudín | poo-**DEAN** |
| Rice | Arroz | ah-**ROHS** |
| Rolls | Panecillos | pan-nay-**SEE**-yos |
| Sorbet | Sorbete | sor-**BAY**-tay |
| Spaghetti | Espagueti | ace-pa-**GAY**-tee |
| Toast | Pan tostado | pahn toes-**TA**-doe |
| Whole grain bread | Pan integral | pahn een-tay-**GRAL** |

**Para Practicar:**

1. Name items on the list that you would consider for dessert: _____

   _____

2. Name items that you could have for breakfast: _____

   _____

3. Which items do you consider to be snacks? _____

   _____

4. Name items that found in the pasta family: _____

   _____

5. Which three items are your favorites? _____

   _____

# Cooking Methods, Flavors

Latin American cooking methods vary from country to country, but one thing is certain; many Latinos are looking for healthier ways to prepare their favorite foods. Even though there hasn't been a rush of "fat-free" or sugar-free foods making their way into the ethnic food section of the grocery store, it's only a matter of time. Some tortilla chips; however, are now available in a lighter form, and after all, salsa is only a mixture of tomatoes and fresh vegetables. In moderation, this makes a tasty, south-of-the-border treat. Americans eat so much salsa every year that more of it is sold now than catsup!

| English | Español | Guide |
|---|---|---|
| Baked | Al orno | al **OR**-no |
| Bitter | Amargo | ah-**MAR**-go |
| Boiled | Hervido | air-**V**-doe |
| Breaded | Empanado | m-pa-**NA**-doe |
| Broiled | Asado | ah-**SA**-doe |
| Chopped | Picado | pee-**CA**-doe |
| Cooked | Cocido | co-**SEE**-doe |
| Dry | Seco | **SAY**-co |
| Fat-free | Sin grasa | seen **GRA**-sa |
| Fresh | Fresco | **FRAYS**-co |
| Fried | Frito | **FREE**-toe |
| Frozen | Congelado | con-hey-**LA**-doe |
| Grilled | A la parilla | ah la par-**E**-ya |
| Microwaved | Cocido en microondas | co-**SEE**-doe n me-crow-**OON**-das |
| Peeled | Pelado | pay-**LA**-doe |
| Raw | Crudo | **CREW**-doe |
| Ripe | Maduro | ma-**DOO**-row |
| Roasted | Asado | ah-**SA**-doe |
| Rotten | Podrido | poe-**DREE**-do |
| Salty | Salado | sa-**LA**-doe |
| Sautéed | Salteado | sal-tay-**AH**-doe |
| Sliced | Rebanado | ray-ba-**NA**-doe |

| English | Español | Guide |
|---------|---------|-------|
| Sour | Agrio | ah-**GREE**-oh |
| Spicy | Picante | pee-**CAHN**-tay |
| Steamed | Cocido al vapor | co-**SEE**-doe al va-**POOR** |
| Stewed | Guisado | gee-**SA**-doe |
| Sweet | Dulce | **DOOL**-say |

## Ingredients

| English | Español | Guide |
|---------|---------|-------|
| Ingredients | Ingredientes | een-gray-dee-**N**-tays |
| Catsup | Ketchup | **KET**-choop |
| Garlic | Ajo | **AH**-ho |
| Herb | Hierba | e-**AIR**-baa |
| Mayonnaise | Mayonesa | ma-yo-**NAY**-sa |
| Mustard | Mostaza | mo-**STA**-sa |
| Oil | Aceite | ah-**SAY**-tay |
| Olive oil | Aceite de oliva | ah-**SAY**-tay day oh-**LEE**-va |
| Pepper | Pimienta | pee-me-**N**-ta |
| Salad dressing | Aderezo | ah-day-**RAY**-so |
| Salt | Sal | sal |
| Sauce | Salsa | **SAL**-sa |
| Spice | Especia | ace-**PAY**-see-ah |
| Sugar | Azúcar | ah-**SUE**-car |
| Vinegar | Vinagre | vee-**NAY**-gray |

### Para Practicar:

Name the spices that you use most often in your home:

_____

# Around Town

Common places around town can provide you with great practice opportunities. The next time you go out to run errands, check the list below. Where are you going? Make a numbered list of the places you intend to go. Now you can practice two important sets of vocabulary at the same time. You can also think about grouping this vocabulary into logical sets. Which places involve travel? Which places involve recreation? Think about the places you go most often. Now, let's get going!

| English | Español | Guide |
|---|---|---|
| Airport | Aeropuerto | ah-eh-row-poo-**AIR**-toe |
| Bakery | Panadería | pan-ah-day-**REE**-ah |
| Bank | Banco | **BAN**-co |
| Barber shop | Peluquería | pay-loo-kay-**REE**-ah |
| Beauty salon | Salón de belleza | sa-**LAWN** day bay-**YEA**-sa |
| Church | Iglesia | e-**GLAY**-see-ah |
| City hall | Municipio | moon-knee-**SEE**-p-oh |
| Fire department | Departamento de bomberos | day-par-ta-**MEN**-toe day bom-**BAY**-rows |
| Florist | Florería | floor-ray-**REE**-ah |
| Gas station | Gasolinera | gas-so-lee-**NAY**-rah |
| Grocery store | Grosería | gros-eh-**REE**-ah |
| Hospital | Hospital | os-p-**TAL** |
| Hotel | Hotel | oh-**TEL** |
| Jewelry store | Joyería | hoy-eh-**REE**-ah |
| Laundromat | Lavandería | la-van-day-**REE**-an |
| Library | Biblioteca | b-lee-oh-**TECK**-ah |
| Market | Mercado | mare-**CA**-doe |
| Movie theatre | Cine | **SEEN**-nay |
| Museum | Museo | moo-**SAY**-oh |
| Park | Parque | **PAR**-kay |

| English | Español | Guide |
|---|---|---|
| Pharmacy | Farmacia | far-**MA**-see-ah |
| Police station | Estación de policía | es-ta-see-**ON** day po-lee-**SEE**-ah |
| Post office | Correo | core-**A**-oh |
| Restaurant | Restaurante | res-tower-**AHN**-tay |
| School | Escuela | es-coo-**A**-la |
| Shoe store | Zapatería | sa-pa-tay-**REE**-ah |
| Store | Tienda | t-**N**-da |
| Super market | Super Mercado | soo-**PEAR** mare-**CA**-doe |
| Theatre | Teatro | tay-**AH**-trow |
| Train station | Estación de tren | es-ta-see-**ON** day tren |
| Subway | Metro | **MAY**-tro |

## Para Practicar:

1. Where could you get a haircut? _____

2. Name places which feature city, state or federal services: _____
   _____

3. Name places where travel takes place: _____
   _____

4. Name places you could go for a night out: _____
   _____

5. Name places where you could shop: _____
   _____

6. Where could you "check in" for a night: _____

# Giving Directions

The ability to give directions in *español* is one of the most practical skills you can have. It adds to your conversational ability and it's a skill you will use over and over again. Slowly, you can start to learn this important vocabulary by knowing simple things, such as the four directions: north, south, east and west. Then, add turns like right and left. Before you know it, you'll be able to give directions to places around town and in your office. This is also easy vocabulary to practice because you can work on it anywhere you go!

| English | Español | Guide |
|---|---|---|
| Where is it? | ¿Dónde está? | **DON**-day ace-**TA** |
| North | Norte | **NOR**-tay |
| South | Sur | **SUE**-er |
| East | Este | **ACE**-tay |
| West | Oeste | oh-**ACE**-tay |
| Above | Encima | n-**SEE**-ma |
| Aisle | Pasillo | pa-**SEE**-yo |
| Avenue | Avenida | ah-ven-**KNEE**-da |
| Behind | Detrás | day-**TRAHS** |
| Down | Abajo | ah-**BAA**-ho |
| Here | Aquí | ah-**KEY** |
| In front of | En frente de | n **FREN**-tay day |
| Inside | Adentro | ah-**DEN**-tro |
| Near | Cerca | **CER**-ca |
| Next to | Al lado de | al **LA**-doe day |
| Outside | Afuera | ah-foo-**AIR**-ah |
| Over there | Allá | ah-**YA** |
| Straight ahead | Adelante | ah-day-**LAN**-tay |
| Street | Calle | **CA**-yea |
| There | Allí | ah-**YE** |
| To the left | A la izquierda | ah la ees-key-**AIR**-dah |
| Turn | Doble | **DOE**-blay |
| To the right | A la derecha | ah la day-**RAY**-cha |
| Up | Arriba | ah-**REE**-ba |

# Traveling from Place to Place

Traveling to exotic locations in Latin America is becoming more and more popular, and it's easy to see why. Trips to Mexico, Central and South America can be very reasonably priced. By air, it doesn't take long to reach an amazing destination. In Latin America there are so many fantastic choices for adventurous travelers. You could go where the jungle meets the sea and experience the endless, pristine beaches of Costa Rica. Perhaps you would prefer to visit Peru's ancient Andean cities built by the Inca. Then again, if modern cities are more your style, you could go to Buenos Aires, Caracas or Mexico City. No matter where you travel, there will be much to do and see, not to mention all the people you will talk to. To hit the road running when you arrive, the following is a list of handy vocabulary that you will need the minute you step off your flight.

| English | Español | Guide |
|---|---|---|
| Airline | Aerolínea | ah-eh-row-**LEAN**-nay-ah |
| Airplane | Avión | ah-v-**ON** |
| Airport | Aeropuerto | ah-eh-row-poo-**AIR**-toe |
| Aisle | Pasillo | pa-**SEE**-yo |
| Arrival | Llegada | yea-**GA**-da |
| Barrage claim | Reclamo de equipaje | ray-**CLAM**-oh day eh-key-**PA**-hey |
| Bathroom | Baño Servicio | **BAHN**-yo ser-**V**-see-oh |
| Bus | Autobús | ow-toe-**BOOS** |
| Bus station | Estación de autobuses | es-sta-see-**ON** day ow-toe-**BOOS**-ace |
| Car | Carro | **CA**-row |
| Carry-on-baggage | Equipaje de mano | eh-key-**PA**-hey day **MA**-no |
| Customs | Aduana | ah-do-**AHN**-na |
| Departure/Exit/Gate | Salida | sa-**LEE**-da |
| Destination | Destinación | des-t-na-see-**ON** |

| English | Español | Guide |
|---------|---------|-------|
| Flight | Vuelto | voo-**EL**-toe |
| Lost and found | Oficina de objetos perdidos | oh-fee-**SEEN**-na day ob-**HEY**-toes pear-**D**-dose |
| Money exchange | Cambio | **CAM**-b-oh |
| Reservation | Reserva | ray-**SER**-va |
| Row | Fila | **FEE**-la |
| Seat | Asiento | ah-see-**N**-toe |
| Security | Seguridad | say-goo-ree-**DAD** |
| Taxi | Taxi | **TAX**-e |
| Terminal | Terminal | ter-me-**NAL** |
| Ticket | Boleto | bow-**LAY**-toe |
| Transportation | Transportación | trans-por-ta-see-**ON** |
| Train station | Estación de tren | es-sta-see-**ON** day tren |
| Subway | Metro | **MAY**-tro |

## Para Practicar:

*Match the following terms.*

1. _____ Money exchange      A. Vuelto

2. _____ Aisle      B. Boleto

3. _____ Flight      C. Reclamo de equipaje

4. _____ Baggage Claim      D. Cambio

5. _____ Customs      E. Salida

6. _____ Ticket      F. Aduana

7. _____ Exit      G. Pasillo

*Key: 1. D  2. G.  3. A  4. C  5. F  6. B  7. E*

# At Your Hotel

Whether you are traveling in the United States or in Latin America, you could run into Spanish-speaking personnel in or around your hotel. At most hotels, large or small, the staff tends to be extremely diverse. This is an asset to the hotel's management because the staff can give great service to guests from all over the world. Some global hotel chains strive to make their personnel as diverse as the United Nations! There's no doubt that somewhere along the way, you will be glad that you can speak Spanish. Knowing how to speak with the key people, who make the hotel run smoothly, can be an important key to having a great stay. It's also a great way to meet people from around the world. Listed below are the most common areas you will find at your hotel.

| English | Español | Guide |
|---|---|---|
| Ball room | Salón de baile | sa-**LAWN** day **BUY**-lay |
| Bar | Bar | bar |
| Beach | Playa | **PLY**-ya |
| Concierge | Conserje | con-**SER**-hey |
| Conference room | Sala de reunión | **SA**-la day ray-un-knee-**ON** |
| Courtyard | Patio | **PA**-t-oh |
| Elevator | Ascensor | ah-sen-**SOAR** |
| Entrance | Entrada | n-**TRA**-da |
| Exit | Salida | sa-**LEE**-da |
| Exercise room | Salón de ejercicio | sa-**LAWN** day ay-hair-**SEE**-see-o |
| Fountain | Fuente | foo-**N**-tay |
| Hallway | Corredor | core-ray-**DOOR** |
| Game room | Salón de juegos | sa-**LAWN** day who-**WAY**-goes |
| Garden | Jardín | har-**DEAN** |
| Gift shop | Tienda de regalos | t-**N**-da day ray-**GAL**-ohs |
| Golf course | Campo de golf | **CAM**-po day golf |
| Guest room | Habitación | ah-bee-ta-see-**ON** |
| Gym | Gimnasio | him-**NA**-see-oh |
| Laundry | Lavandería | la-van-dare-**REE**-ah |

| English | Español | Guide |
|---|---|---|
| Lobby | Vestíbulo | vase-**TEE**-boo-lo |
| Office | Oficina | oh-fee-**SEEN**-na |
| Parking lot | Estacionamiento | ace-ta-see-oh-na-me-**N**-toe |
| Pool | Piscina<br>Alberca | pee-**SEEN**-na<br>al-**BEAR**-ca |
| Restaurant | Restaurante | ray-sta-our-**RANT**-tay |
| Spa | Centro de salud<br>y belleza | **CEN**-tro day sa-**LEWD**<br>e bay-**YEA**-sa |
| Tennis court | Cancha de tenis | **CAN**-cha day **TAY**-knees |

## Para Practicar:

*March the following terms:*

1. _____ Elevator

2. _____ Lobby

3. _____ Restaurant

4. _____ Gift shop

5. _____ Conference Room

6. _____ Guest Room

7. _____ Exercise Room

8. _____ Spa

9. _____ Pool

10. _____ Parkinglot

A. Restaurante

B. Habitación

C. Sala de reunión

D. Centro de salud y belleza

E. Salón de ejercicio

F. Piscina or Alberca

G. Ascensor

H. Estacionamiento

I. Tienda de regalos

J. Vestíbulo

*Key: 1. G  2. J  3. A  4. I  5. C  6. B  7. E  8. D  9. F  10. H*

# In Your Hotel Room

It doesn't matter if you travel frequently on business or occasionally with your family, there's nothing worse than checking into your hotel room to find that something's wrong. Even little things can cause big problems if you don't know how to ask for what you need or explain "*el problema*." Have the towels in your room been overlooked? Is a light bulb out at the desk where you need to work? Something as simple as a burned out battery in the TV's remote control can be the straw that broke the tired traveler's back— especially if you are traveling with "*niños*." For smooth sailing on your next trip, learn the words for these common items found in hotel rooms and, no matter what the problem is, you'll be able to solve it.

| English | Español | Guide |
|---|---|---|
| Air conditioning | Aire acondicionado | **EYE**-ray ah-con-dee-see-oh-**NA**-doe |
| Bath tub | Bañera | ban-**YEA**-rah |
| Bathroom | Baño | **BAN**-yo |
| Battery | Pila | **P**-la |
| Bed | Cama | **KA**-ma |
| Bed spread | Colcha | **COAL**-cha |
| Cabinet | Armario | arm-**MARE**-ree-oh |
| Chair | Silla | **SEE**-ya |
| Clock | Reloj | **RAY**-low |
| Curtain | Cortina | cor-**TEE**-na |
| Desk | Escritorio | es-cree-**TOR**-ree-oh |
| Door | Puerta | pooh-**AIR**-ta |
| Floor | Piso | **PEE**-so |
| Heater | Calentador | ca-lent-ta-**DOOR** |
| Jacuzzi | Jacuzzi® | Jacuzzi |
| Lamp | Lámpara | **LAMB**-pa-rah |
| Light | Luz | loose |
| Mirror | Espejo | ace-**PAY**-jo |
| Remote control | Control remoto | con-**TROL** ray-**MO**-toe |

| English | Español | Guide |
|---|---|---|
| Sheet | Sábana | **SA**-baa-na |
| Sink | Lavabo | la-**VAH**-bow |
| Smoke detector | Detector de humo | day-tec-**TOR** day **OO**-mo |
| Table | Mesa | **MAY**-sa |
| Telephone | Teléfono | tay-**LAY**-foe-no |
| Television | Televisor | tay-lay-vee-**SOAR** |
| Trash | Basura | bah-**SUE**-rah |
| Towel | Toalla | toe-**EYE**-ya |
| Wall | Pared | pah-**RED** |
| Water | Agua | **AH**-gua |
| Window | Ventana | ven-**TAN**-na |
| Whirlpool tub | Bañera de hidromasaje | bahn-**YAIR**-rah day eed-row-ma-**SA**-hey |

## Para Practicar:

*Match the following words:*

1. _____ Sheets

2. _____ Bed

3. _____ Bathtub

4. _____ Trash

5. _____ Telephone

6. _____ Heater

7. _____ Remote control

8. _____ Towel

A. Basura

B. Calentador

C. Toalla

D. Sábana

E. Control remoto

F. Bañera

G. Cama

H. Teléfono

*Key: 1. D 2. G 3. F 4. A 5. H 6. B 7. E 8. C*

# Talking with the Housekeeping Staff

Recently an associate told me about a situation he found himself in on a business trip. Early one morning a member of the hotel's housekeeping staff knocked at his door. As she entered the room and began her cleaning routine, she said, "*Buenos días, señor.*" Mike, who is a savvy, environmentally conscious traveler, was staying at the hotel one more day, so he didn't want the housekeeper to change the sheets. Seeing that Mike was trying to tell her something, the housekeeper, who didn't speak *inglés*, handed him a card on which the phrases below were written. Mike thought the phrases were so practical, he asked for a copy when he checked out. Since he shared them with us, we want to share them with you.

| English | Español | Guide |
|---------|---------|-------|
| Please clean the room. | Favor de limpiar la habitación. | fa-**VOR** day leem-p-**ARE** la ah-b-ta-see-**ON** |
| No service, please. | No servicio, por favor. | no ser-**V**-see-oh pour fa-**VOR** |
| Just trash | Sola basura | **SO**-la ba-**SUE**-rah |
| Just towels | Sola toallas | **SO**-la toe-**EYE**-yas |
| I need more regular coffee. | Necesito más café regular. | nay-say-**SEE**-toe mas ca-**FAY** ray-goo-**LAR** |
| I need more decaffeinated coffee.   Coffee in the green packet | Necesito más café descafinado.   Café en el paquete verde | nay-say-**SEE**-toe mas ca-**FAY** des-ca-fee-**NA**-doe ca-**FAY** in el pa-**KET**-tay **VER**-day |
| I need extra towels. | Necesito más toallas. | nay-say-**SEE**-toe mas toe-**EYE**-yas |
| Change the sheets. | Cambie las sábanas. | **CAM**-be-a las **SA**-ba-nas |
| Clean the bathroom. | Limpie el baño. | **LEEM**-p-ay el **BAHN**-yo |
| Vacuum the room | Aspire la habitación. | ah-**SPEER**-ay la ah-b-ta-see-**ON** |

| English | Español | Guide |
|---|---|---|
| Come back later. | Regrese más tarde. | ray-**GRES**-ay mas **TAR**-day |
| In 10 minutes | En diez minutos | in d-**ACE** me-**NEW**-toes |
| In 30 minutes | En treinta minutos | in **TRAIN**-ta me-**NEW**-toes |
| In an hour | En una hora | in una **OR**-rah |
| I need more tissue. | Necesito más de papel Kleenex®. | nay-say-**SEE**-toe mas day pa-**PEL** Kleenex® |
| I need more shampoo. | Necesito más champú. | nay-say-**SEE**-toe mas cham-**POO** |
| I need more lotion | Necesito más cremas. | nay-say-**SEE**-toe mas **CRAY**-mas |
| I need more toilet paper | Necesito más papel de baño. | nay-say-**SEE**-toe mas pa-**PEL** day **BAHN**-yo |
| I need more soap | Necesito más jabones | nay-say-**SEE**-toe mas ja-**BOW**-nace |
| I need to talk to a supervisor. | Necesito hablar con un supervisor. | nay-say-**SEE**-toe ah-**BLAR** con sue sue-pear-v-**SOAR** |

## Para Practicar:

Using the phrases in this chapter, what would you say in the following situations?

1. You are just getting out of the shower and you want the housekeeper

   to come back later: _____

2. You only need service in the bathroom:

   _____

3. Your room is out of tissues: _____

# Buying Clothes

No matter where you are, a good sale is hard to pass by. If you're traveling in Latin America, you could very well find yourself at a large flea market or a high-end department store filled with bargains of all sorts. The following vocabulary will help you purchase clothing and find all the best deals and discounts.

¡VENTA!

| English | Español | Guide |
|---------|---------|-------|
| Bathing suit | Traje de baño | **TRAH**-hey day **BAHN**-yo |
| Belt | Cinturón | seen-too-**RHONE** |
| Boots | Botas | **BOW**-tas |
| Dress | Vestido | ves-**T**-doe |
| Gloves | Guantes | goo-**AHN**-tays |
| Hat | Sombrero | som-**BRAY**-row |
| Jacket | Chaqueta | cha-**KAY**-ta |
| Jeans | Jeans Vaqueros | Jeans va-**KAY**-rows |
| Overcoat | Abrigo | ah-**BREE**-go |
| Pants | Pantalones | pan-ta-**LONE**-ace |
| Pajamas | Pijamas | p-**HA**-mas |
| Raincoat | Impermeable | eem-pear-may-**AH**-blay |
| Robe | Bata | **BA**-ta |
| Sandals | Sandalias | san-**DAL**-e-ahs |
| Scarf | Bufanda | boo-**FAHN**-da |
| Shirt | Camisa | ca-**ME**-sa |
| Shoes | Zapatos | sa-**PA**-toes |
| Shorts | Pantalones cortos | pan-ta-**LONE**-ace **CORE**-toes |
| Skirt | Falda | **FALL**-da |
| Sneakers | Tenis | **TAY**-knees |
| Socks | Calcetines | cal-say-**TEEN**-ace |
| Suit | Traje | **TRAH**-hey |
| Sweater | Suéter | sue-**A**-ter |
| Tie | Corbata | core-**BA**-ta |

| English | Español | Guide |
|---|---|---|
| T-shirt | Camiseta | ca-me-**SAY**-ta |
| Umbrella | Paraguas | **PA**-ra-**AH**-goo-wahs |
| Underwear | Ropa interior | **ROW**-pa een-tay-ree-**OR** |
| Vest | Chaleco | cha-**LAY**-co |

## Para Practicar:

1. Name items you could use at the beach: _____

_____

2. Name items you could use when it's cold: _____

_____

3. Name the parts of a man's suit: _____

_____

4. Name items you could wear in the summer: _____

_____

5. Which items do you consider to be accessories? _____

_____

6. What items would you use in the rain? _____

_____

7. What items could you wear playing tennis? _____

_____

# Sizes & Sales

| English | Español | Guide |
|---|---|---|
| I need a size | Necesito un tamaño | nay-say-**SEE**-toe oon ta-**MAHN**-yo |
| Small | Pequeño | pay-**CAIN**-yo |
| Medium | Mediano | may-d-**AH**-no |
| Large | Grande | **GRAHN**-day |
| Extra large | Extra grande | **X**-tra **GRAHN**-day |
| I like it. | Me gusta. | may **GOO**-sta |
| It fits. | Me queda. | may **KAY**-da |
| It doesn't fit. | No me queda bien. | no may **KAY**-da b-**N** |
| It's small. | Es pequeño. | es pay-**CAIN**-yo |
| It's tight. | Es apretado. | es ah-pray-**TA**-doe |
| It's short. | Es corto. | es **CORE**-toe |
| It's long. | Es largo. | es **LAR**-go |

| English | Español | Guide |
|---|---|---|
| Are there any sales? | ¿Hay ventas? | eye **VEIN**-tas |
| Are there discounts? | ¿Hay descuentos? | eye des-coo-**WAYNE**-toes |
| Is someone helping you? | ¿Los están atendiendo? | los ace-**TAN** ah-ten-knee-**N**-doe |
| What would you like? | ¿Qué desea? | kay day-**SAY**-ah |
| What are you looking for? | ¿Para qué está buscando? | **PA**-rah kay ace-**TA** boos-**CAHN**-doe |
| I'm looking for a _____ | Estoy buscando un (una) _____. | ace-**TOY** boos-**CAHN**-doe oon/**OO**-na |

# Colors

Now, let's put it all together. Colors are adjectives, and as you learned in the chapter covering descriptions, they are treated differently in Spanish than they are in English. First, they will normally be positioned after the noun they modify, not in front of it. Next, look for spelling changes. If the color ends with the letter "o" or an "a," change it's spelling, depending on the category of noun it's describing. Adjectives paired with feminine nouns usually end with an "a," and adjectives paired with masculine nouns usually end with an "o." If the word you are describing is plural, the adjective should be plural, too. As usual, you will find a few exceptions. Language is a lot like people. We don't always follow the rules and neither does it! When the color doesn't end in either an "a" or an "o," like the Spanish word blue or "*azul*," it doesn't change its spelling. That's because it doesn't end with a vowel. This principle of Spanish seems complicated to everyone at first, but with practice, you'll get the hang of it. The matching endings of Spanish adjectives and nouns give it a lilting, musical quality. That's what makes *español* one of the world's most beautiful languages.

| English | Español | Guide |
|---------|---------|-------|
| Red | Rojo | **ROW**-ho |
| Orange | Naranja | na-**RAHN**-ha |
| Yellow | Amarillo | ah-ma-**REE**-yo |
| Blue | Azul | ah-**SUL** |
| Green | Verde | **VER**-day |
| Purple | Morado | more-**AH**-doe |
| Black | Negro | **NAY**-grow |
| Pink | Rosa | **ROW**-sa |
| Lavender | Lavanda | la-**VAHN**-da |
| Pale | Claro | **CLAH**-row |
| Dark | Oscuro | oh-**SKOOR**-oh |
| White | Blanco | **BLAHN**-co |
| Gold | Oro | **OH**-row |
| Silver | Plata | **PLAH**-ta |
| Copper | Cobre | **CO**-bray |
| Gray | Gris | Grease |

# One for the Road: Phrases to Use Any Time

Obviously, conversation is made up of more than just lists of words. It will take practice and determination for you to achieve free-flowing conversation in a language that's new to you. Learning Spanish is a slow and steady process for adults. It could take several months before you begin to "think" in Spanish, so don't expect to achieve native speaker speed over night! There will be times when you feel like you can't remember anything you've studied. That's natural. It happens to everyone. Try not to be discouraged. The rewards you'll receive from learning to speak Spanish are far greater than a little bit of frustration. If you keep working, it won't be long before you'll have a break-through. Learning Spanish is a lot like eating a great steak. You don't want to rush it. Cut each bite of your Spanish, chew it over carefully and savor each morsel. Moving along at a slower pace will help you retain what you learn longer.

Spanish is a language that has loads of zest and flair. It is punctuated with single words and short phrases that can really express a lot of sentiment. The next time you have an opportunity to observe native speakers, listen carefully. You may hear them switch from English to Spanish, depending on what they are saying. And, you might hear them use any of the "one-liners" listed below. Phrases like these add spice to your conversation. Use the following list to help you take your conversational skills to the next level.

| English | Español | Guide |
|---------|---------|-------|
| Are you sure? | ¿Está seguro? (a) | ace-**TA** say-**GOO**-row |
| Excellent! | ¡Excelente! | x-say-**LENT**-tay |
| Fantastic! | ¡Fantástico! | fan-**TA**-stee-co |
| Good idea. | Buena idea. | boo-**A**-na e-**DAY**-ah |
| Happy birthday! | ¡Feliz cumpleaños! | fay-**LEASE** coom-play-**AHN**-yos |
| Have a nice day. | Tenga un buen día. | **TEN**-ga un boo-**WAYNE** **DEE**-ah |

| English | Español | Guide |
|---|---|---|
| I agree. | De acuerdo. | day ah-coo-**AIR**-doe |
| I believe so. | Creo que sí. | **CRAY**-oh kay **SEE** |
| I'm so glad. | Me alegro. | may ah-**LAY**-gro |
| I'll be right back. | ¡Ahora vengo! | ah-**OR**-ah **VEIN**-go |
| I'm leaving now. | ¡Ya me voy! | ya may **VOY** |
| That's OK. | Está bien. | es-**TA** b-**N** |
| It's important. | Es importante. | es eem-pour-**TAHN**-tay |
| It's serious. | Es grave. | es **GRA**-vay |
| It's possible. | Es posible | es po-**SEE**-blay |
| Like this? | ¿Así? | ah-**SEE** |
| Maybe. | Quizás. | key-**SAHS** |
| Me, neither | Yo tampoco. | yo tam-**PO**-co |
| Me, too | Yo también. | yo tam-b-**N** |
| More or less | Más o menos. | mas oh **MAY**-nos |
| Really? | ¿De veras? | day **VER**-ahs |
| Sure | ¡Claro! | **CLA**-row |
| That depends. | Depende. | day-**PEN**-day |
| We'll see you. | Nos vemos. | nos **VAY**-mos |

**Para Practicar:**

1. Name some phrases that could accompany "adiós": _____

   _____

2. Name a few words you could say when something is really great:

   _____

3. Name a few things you could say when things are going well:

   _____

# Typing in Spanish with Microsoft Word
## Inserting an International Character with Shortcut Keys

When you need to type letters with accent marks or use Spanish punctuation, you will use keys that you have probably never used before! Actually, you are composing characters using the control key. It is located on the bottom row of keys. You will see that it is such an important key that there is one on both sides. It keeps the computer from moving forward one space so that the accent goes on top of the letter instead of beside it.

Always remember to hold the control key down first. It will be the key to your success in word processing Spanish. With a little practice these keys will become a normal part of your word processing skills.

Simple note: If using Microsoft Word®, use the menu command Insert>Symbol.

| To insert | Press |
|---|---|
| á, é, í, ó, ú, ý Á, É, Í, Ó, Ú, Ý | CTRL+' (APOSTROPHE), *the letter* |
| â, ê, î, ô, û Â, Ê, Î, Ô, Û | CTRL+SHIFT+^ (CARET), *the letter* |
| ã, ñ, õ Ã, Ñ, Õ | CTRL+SHIFT+~ (TILDE), *the letter* |
| ä, ë, ï, ö, ü, ÿ Ä, Ë, Ï, Ö, Ü, Ÿ | CTRL+SHIFT+: (COLON), *the letter* |
| ¿ | ALT+CTRL+SHIFT+? |
| ¡ | ALT+CTRL+SHIFT+! |

# Practicing What You Learned

Practice is an important part of the language learning process. The more you include practice time in your daily routine, the more comfortable and fluent you will become. There is no easy way to practice. It just takes time. The key to practicing Spanish is to set realistic goals. Don't let the language learning process become overwhelming to you. Yes, there is a lot to learn, and it will take some time. But, by setting realistic goals, you have a greater chance of sticking with it. Each of us have different learning styles, so find out what works best for you and break the material down into small pieces. Some of us learn best by listening. Others need to write the words and phrases in order to visualize them. Generally the more of your senses that you involve in the learning process, the faster you will retain the information. So, focus and practice one thing at a time. It's doing the little things that will make the greatest difference in the long run. Working five minutes every day on your Spanish is *mucho* better than trying to put in an hour of practice time only once each week. Consistency in your practice is critical.

Here are some practice tips that have worked for me and others, who have participated in *SpeakEasy's Survival Spanish* programs over the last few years. Start practicing your Spanish first thing in the morning while you are in the shower. Yes, while you are in the shower! It's private time that you have to focus on the day ahead. Set the tone for your day by practicing your Spanish. You will be more likely to think about it and continue to practice throughout the day if you start in the shower. While you shampoo, run through the Spanish alphabet or count up to 100. I did this every day while I was in college and it really worked for me. Practice words that use the Spanish "r" sound, like *burrito* and *señor*. This will help you in this important aspect of the Spanish sound system. Another reason why I say practice in the shower is that the hot water and steam will help to warm up your vocal cords and facial muscles. That is very important to practicing any language. Because Spanish requires the use of the muscles around your mouth and lips, this should feel great. And, when you are in the shower alone, you don't have to worry about what anyone else hears or thinks about your Spanish. Take advantage of every spare second you have.  After all, once you step out of the shower, it's an all out race to the office.

Another great place to practice your Spanish is in your car. Depending on my class schedule, there are times when I need to learn as many as 50 new words and phrases each week.  If I didn't break this into reasonable pieces, this would be a tremendous task!   So, I try to prepare myself for the task ahead.  Try this and see if it will work for you.  On Sunday night when you prepare for the week ahead, take a sticky note and write ten words or phrases that you would like to learn during the week. Take the note and put in on the center of your car's steering wheel.  When you are stopped at traffic lights, scan your "hot" list and say the words out loud.  Do this exercise only when you are stopped in el *tráfico*!  My *amiga*, Dorothy, was practicing in Rock Hill, SC on her way to a *restaurante Mexicano*, but she wasn't stopped at the light.  She ran through it without thinking and was involved in an *accidente*.  She was very lucky to escape injury, but her *carro* was a total loss.  So, make *sure* to only practice when you are stopped.  But, think about it.  If you add up all the time that you waste when you are stopped at traffic lights, you will find an additional 5 to ten minutes every day to practice.

Numbers make a great set of vocabulary words to practice in your car. This is such an important set of vocabulary.  You just can't practice them enough.  Most professionals have to ask for telephone numbers, social security numbers or even employee identification numbers every day.  Even if you forget to make a list of on-the-job words and phrases that you need to work on for the week, you can still work with numbers.  Look around for numbers when your car is stopped.  Start by looking at the license tag of the car in front of you.   Practice the alphabet and your numbers by repeating the license tag *en español*.  If there isn't a car in front of you, look for billboards or street signs that contain numbers.  After all, numbers are everywhere.  Try to increase your speed as your practice.  *Los números* will be said to at you with lightening speed, so prepare yourself by practicing them often.

It's important to vary your practice routine in the car.  After all, everyone gets bored with the same workout at the gym.  The same thing will happen to you when you practice your Spanish, if you don't find other tools to help you.  Find good language tapes and CD's to help you develop an "ear" for Spanish.  Currently SpeakEasy Communications, Inc. offers CD's with pronunciation guides for construction, healthcare, and warehouse personnel.  Soon, we will be offering products for employers, apartment managers, pharmacists, and social workers.  However, you can find many good products now at local bookstores or on-line with the major book store chains.  Also, find out if there are Spanish language radio stations in your area.  That is a great way to practice and it won't cost you any money.

The internet is also a great resource when it comes to practicing your Spanish.  The web is loaded with instructional sites, specialized dictionaries and chat rooms.  All you need to do is get out there and surf! One of my favorite sites is http://www.spanish.about.com.  Here you can find a wealth of information about the Spanish language and Latin American countries.  There is different information every day.  Now, it even features an on-line Spanish language newsletter that you can subscribe to.  These are great, free tools to help you vary your practice routine.  The internet can also help. If you need a quick and easy translation, go to http://www.freetranslation.com.  It's a big help.  Just type in the phrase you need translated into Spanish and click.  A reasonable translation will be right at your fingertips.  But, take this word of caution.  The computer only knows what you tell it!  Check your phrase for sentence fragments and misspelled words.  If you have typos in your English phrase, the machine can't make Spanish heads or tails out of it!  This sort of "quickie" translation should never be used for official company documents.  Pay to have them translated by a professional.  It is an investment that will save you and your *compañía* lots of embarrassment in the long run.

Even though most of your language practice will be done *solo*, having a practice partner at work is a great idea.  Learning together can be much more fun that working alone.  If you have a practice *amigo*, you can work on your interviewing skills together.  Take the basic information interview found on page 20 for example.  Make blank copies of this important page.  Get your friend to make up information for a new Hispanic "employee".  Give that person a new name, address, telephone, social security number, and nationality.  Then, get together and practice.  Take the blank form and start by asking the questions.  Get your practice partner to give you the new answers, and see if you are able to fill out the form completely without using English. Let the use of English be your only limitation, however. Use quick reference guides, body language or anything else that will help you get the information. Then, switch roles. Practice interviewing every week but make up new information each time. After all, you will be asking the same questions over and over, but the information the new employee tells you will always be different. Have fun with this exercise. Go out to eat and run this exercise while you relax. The first time you do it, you will feel awkward and slow. The next time you will be more comfortable and you will be faster. The more often you practice this *importante* skill the better and more efficient you will become.

In addition to CD's, tapes and radio stations, Spanish language newspapers in your area are also super resources to help you learn. Look for them in Mexican restaurants or at your local grocery store. Many of them are even free or *gratis*. Spanish language newspapers are important because learning languages as an adult is different from acquiring them in childhood. As an adult, one of the first skills you will accomplish in the target language is reading. When you are reading, you can take all the time you need. You won't have the pressure of trying to translate what is being said to you, and you won't have to worry about your accent or grammar in making a reply. When you pick up a Spanish language newspaper, look for all the English – Spanish matches first. These "cognates" will help you build your vocabulary *pronto*! First, try to translate for the "gist" not for word for word meaning. That can be very frustrating and time consuming when you are just starting. Have fun! Start by look at the advertisements and translating those. Then, work yourself up to longer articles. Also, look for sections on your particular area of expertise. Many newspapers include a business, health, or sports section. You will often find articles there that can help you on the job. And, if you are looking for Spanish-speaking employees at your firm, the Spanish language newspaper in your area is a great way to advertise. You can find my favorite local paper at http://www.lanoticia.com. Once again you can go on-line to find the major daily newspapers in almost all of 18 Latin American countries. This web site contains links to newspapers and magazines in a variety of Latin American countries: http://www.lib.utsa.edu/Instruction/helpsheets/pubs.html. To me, it's interesting to read articles from papers in other countries. You can really see and appreciate a wealth of different opinions on a variety of topics from US foreign policy to movies. We can often learn a lot about ourselves from how others see us. It all leaves me wondering. What did we do without the internet to keep us connected?

I hope you find this book and the study tips it contains to be a great resource for you as you conquer on-the-job Spanish. Just remember: you are not alone. According to *USA Today*, there are 35.3 million people now who speak Spanish in the United States. It is rapidly becoming the second business language in America. So, let your Spanish-speaking employees and friends help you learn. You will find that they are as eager to learn English as you are to learn Spanish, and before you know it you will be ready to move into other conversational areas. One of my favorite places to practice is the Mexican restaurant nearest my ***casa***. The staff there is always willing to teach me some slang or answer my questions. This is a great place for you to make a friendly ***conexión***!

It's also important to remember that you didn't learn English overnight, and the same thing is true for Spanish. Learning Spanish is like gaining any other skill. It takes patience and discipline. For me, there is a little stubbornness thrown in, too! Don't give up and don't expect to be perfect in your Spanish. Even in English, we make mistakes all the time. If we don't speak our own language perfectly, how can we possibly think we can be perfect in another language? It's only natural for you to make mistakes. That is how we learn! Just laugh about it, learn from it, and move on. After all, when you successfully communicate an idea in another language and someone understands what you are trying to say, that's ***magnífico***! Just set reasonable goals and practice daily, then you will be able to survive in Spanish!

1. Learn words you use the most first.
2. Focus on 10 words each week.
3. Practice 10 minutes every day.
4. Label items with post-it notes.
5. Practice at work.

# About the Author

## Myelita Melton, MA

Myelita Melton, founder of SpeakEasy Communications, remembers the first time she heard a "foreign" language. She knew from that moment what she wanted to do with her life. "Since I was always the kid in class that talked too much," Myelitia says, "I figured it would be a good idea to learn more than one language- that way I could talk to a lot more people!" After high school, she studied in Mexico at the *Instituto de Filológica Hispánica* and completed both her BA and MA in French and Curriculum Design at Appalachian State University in Boone, NC. She has studied French, Spanish, Italian, and German.

"Lita's" unique career includes classroom instruction and challenging corporate experience. She has won several national awards, including a prestigious *Rockefeller* scholarship. In 1994 she was named to *Who's Who among Outstanding Americans*. Myelita's corporate experience includes owning a television production firm, working with NBC's Spanish news division, *Canal de Noticias,* and Charlotte's PBS affiliate WTVI. In her spare time, she continues to broadcast with WDAV, a National Public Radio station near Lake Norman in North Carolina where she lives.

**MEMBER**

**NATIONAL SPEAKERS ASSOCIATION**

In 1997 Myelita started SpeakEasy Communications to offer industry specific Spanish instruction in North Carolina. The company is now the nation's leader in Spanish training, offering over 30 *SpeakEasy Spanish*™ programs and publications to companies, associations, and colleges throughout the US.

Lita is also a member of the National Speaker's Association and the National Council for Continuing Education and Training. Many of her clients say she is the most high-energy, results-oriented speaker they have ever seen. As she travels the country speaking on cultural diversity issues in the workplace and languages, she has truly realized her dream of being able to talk to the world.

HILLSBORO PUBLIC LIBRARIES
Hillsboro, OR
Member of Washington County
COOPERATIVE LIBRARY SERVICES